W9-AAC-488

# Ron Kay's Guide
# to Zion National Park

# Ron Kay's Guide to Zion National Park

Everything You Always Wanted to Know About Zion
National Park But Didn't Know Who to Ask

Ron Kay

THE COUNTRYMAN PRESS
WOODSTOCK, VERMONT

Copyright © 2008 by Ron Kay

First Edition

All rights reserved. No part of this book may be reproduced in any way by electronic
or mechanical means, including information storage and retrieval systems,
without permission in writing from the publisher, except by a reviewer,
who may quote brief passages.

ISBN 978-0-88150-792-8

Cover design by Johnson Design, Inc.
Interior design and composition by S. E. Livingston
Interior photographs by the author
Maps by Kai Huschke, © The Countryman Press

Published by The Countryman Press,
P.O. Box 748, Woodstock, Vermont 05091

Distributed by W.W. Norton & Company, Inc.,
500 Fifth Avenue, New York, NY 10110

Printed in the United States of America

10 9 8 7 6 5 4 3 2 1

*Title page photo: Zion at sunset*

# Dear Readers:

After many years of teaching, guiding, and answering questions from students, hikers, and visitors to Zion National Park, I came to realize a complete information source was not available, and so the idea for this guide came to mind. When looking to discover the beauty and adventure that Zion has to offer, many visitors are overwhelmed by the opportunities of where to look, where to start, and how to best utilize their time.

The purpose of this guide is to help readers experience Zion in a way that will long be remembered. Descriptions of hikes in this book are complete, giving you a feel for the difficulty of the hike, the location of the hike, and what you may encounter while on the hike. Introductory material is designed to give you information about the park and answer the most common questions asked by users of this beautiful area. When visiting a place like Zion, part of the fun is leaving with a sense of fulfillment and fond memories. It is my intent with this guide to make that possible.

Thank you for your purchase of *Ron Kay's Guide To Zion National Park*. I hope you leave Zion with memories that will last a lifetime.

Sincerely,
Ron Kay

# Contents

# Special Notes to My Readers

Only experienced climbers or those with extensive canyoneering experience should attempt canyoneering routes. These routes are not for the general hiker or for those with limited canyoneering training. All route descriptions are general in nature and should not be taken as a step-by-step instruction. Routes can and do change.

I have included a parachute cord under some "Equipment Needed" lists in chapter 7, "Backcountry Canyoneering Route Descriptions," and wish to clarify that unless you are familiar with how to use a parachute cord and have used it in the past to assist you in canyoneering techniques, it should not be used. A parachute cord should never be used as an additional rope or human conveyance. Also, it should be noted that equipment such as ascenders or other devices are needed to maneuver knots in your decent.

Even with the corrections indicated every reader should understand that the routes could change on a moment's notice due to the evolving canyons of Zion National Park. Always check with the Backcountry Office before attempting any outing within the park.

I have provided maps to trail and route locations, however, I would recommend purchasing a topographic map for use when following backcountry or canyoneering routes. When used in conjunction with my guide, you should be able to follow the directions I have provided.

*"It would take more than a lifetime to really know Zion;*
*but in a week you might really know yourself.*
*And that's even better."*

—*Freeman Tilden*

# 1. Introduction and History of Zion

## Welcome to Zion National Park

Zion! A place of safety and refuge. The meaning alone sparks the imagination with wonder and visions of a place like no other. Zion is indeed a place like no other, with cliffs towering above the canyon floor like magnificent temples. Giant monoliths stand as guardians over the canyon and all those who venture through its inspiring beauty. People who visit this majestic land find awe, wonder, and an inner peace unsurpassed by any other place.

This extraordinary landscape will leave you feeling as though you have visited the "Heavenly City of God," a name bestowed upon this place by early settlers. The sedimentary rocks are vivid with colors of red, yellow, purple, green, and rust. The endless erosion of the canyon itself will provide you with a vacation adventure that will be with you for a lifetime. Artists, photographers, researchers, and visitors all agree this is truly a place of refuge. During the course of the day you will see colors, shadows, and a skyline that will exhaust your film supply.

## The Geologic Story of Zion

The creation of Zion National Park began approximately 260 million years ago and consists of four geologic processes: sedimentation, lithification, uplift, and erosion. The beautiful cliffs, towers, and canyons are part of the Colorado Plateau. Zion is located on the very southwest corner of this plateau. Consisting of eight different sedimentary layers, Zion offers a view into our past. Let's take a look at the four geologic processes and what part each played in the creation of Zion National Park.

## Sedimentation

Each visible layer (or formation) found in Zion represents a different environment during deposition. Let's begin with the oldest or bottommost formation found in the park, the Kaibab Formation

### The Kaibab Formation
(Geologic Time Scale: Middle Permian;
Approximate Age: 260 million years)

*Observation Point*

This sedimentary limestone layer began to form when Zion was located about 10 degrees north of the equator. The region was below sea level and on the western edge of the continent. The environment was a shallow sea with a moderately dry landmass to its east. This time frame would have placed Zion in the northern hemisphere, but in a tropical climate. The formation is approximately 550 feet thick.

### The Moenkopi Formation
(Geologic Time Scale: Early Triassic;
Approximate Age: 240 million years)

This sedimentary rock layer, consisting of shales, siltstones, sandstones, gypsum, mudstones, and limestone, began its formation well after the Kaibab formation. The fossils found here are much different, leading us to believe there was a change in the chemistry of the shallow seawater. This formation is recognized by the unique banding appearance sometimes referred to as the bacon strip formation. This banding resulted from a tidal effect in the sea. This formation also shows the gradual receding of the sea as the area becoming more continental. The Moenkopi formation is approximately 1,800 feet thick.

### The Chinle Formation
(Geologic Time Scale: Late Triassic;
Approximate Age: 220 million years)

The Chinle formation shows that a dramatic change had occurred in the environment. The area changed from a sea and tropical type environment to an active volcanic area with lakes and strong-flowing rivers. This formation hosts the petrified wood found in the park. The type of wood found leads us to believe that the waters would have traveled west from the Colorado area, and indeed would have had strong currents in order to carry the wood this far. This formation also contains large amounts of volcanic ash. The volcanic activity may have been triggered by a drift of the continent and crustal movement, pushing the Zion region north and changing the environment to that of a rain forest. The Chinle formation is approximately 500 feet thick.

### The Moenave Formation
(Geologic Time Scale: Late Triassic;
Approximate Age: 210 million years)

The Moenave formation consists of red siltstone on the bottom and pink sandstone on the top. This formation shows the area began as slow/low-energy stream environment depositing silts along the streambeds. The environment changed to fast/high-energy stream discharges carrying and depositing sands. Fish inhabited the streams and ponds; this was also the beginning of the dinosaur era, as demonstrated by the presence of tracks. The Moenave formation is approximately 550 feet thick.

### The Kayenta Formation
(Geologic Time Scale: Early Jurassic;
Approximate Age: 200 million years)

Consisting of siltstones and sandstones, this formation is the wooded, sloping layer just prior to the tall vertical cliffs. The area was a lake or river-type environment with wet summers and dry winters. The larger species of dinosaurs were roaming the land as the continent was beginning its northward drift to the formation of the great desert.

### The Navajo Formation
(Geologic Time Scale: Early Jurassic;
Approximate Age: 190 million years)

The most dramatic of sedimentary formations within Zion are the tall vertical cliffs. A remnant of ancient desert, and void of fossils, this formation tells us of a harsh, sand swept environment. Evidence of this desert region can be found from Wyoming through Utah, continuing into Nevada and on to Southern California. This desert environment would have been similar to the Sahara Desert of today. The sands within Zion however, accumulated to a depth of over 2,500 feet, making it the deepest desert environment in the world. The Navajo sandstone has an average thickness of 2,200 feet.

### Temple Cap Formation
(Geologic Time Scale: Early/Mid Jurassic;
Approximate Age: 180 million years)

Consisting of red mudstone, this formation shows that the vast desert environment changed for a brief time. Streams carrying mud and depositing clay and silts to create a capstone for this desert flooded the area. The desert environment gradually returned, where we find a mixture of sandstone and mudstone as the climate was beginning to change once again. The Temple Cap formation is only about 20–30 feet thick.

### Carmel Formation
(Geologic Time Scale: Mid-Jurassic;
Approximate Age: 160 million years)

This formation shows the continued gradual change from the desert environment to a shallow sea with desert coastlines as the ocean encroached from the west. Red muds are presently covering the sandstone, followed by limestone, showing us that the area began to become inundated by rivers carrying clays and silts. It was eventually covered by the sea, which left behind the limestone. This formation is approximately 850 feet thick.

## Lithification

As you can see, the geologic history of Zion is vast and ever changing. You learned how the formations were created and what the environment was like during each deposition period, But how did all of this mud, ash, and sand turn to stone? The process by which sedimentary deposition becomes stone is referred to as lithification. The transformation begins with the introduction of mineral-carrying waters to the sedimentary deposition. As the water covers the deposits, minerals from the water leach down through the deposition and literally cement the small particles or rock fragments together. The most prominent mineral found in Zion is calcium carbonate—the same mineral you have at home that causes hard water deposits. It is a very strong, tough mineral and does an effective job working as a cementing agent. Imagine this process as the same recipe for making modern-day concrete. If we mix sand, gravel, water, and cement (an artificial mineral), the end result is a man-made rock. This process, combined with successive compression due to layering, turned millions of years of deposition into the rock we see today.

## Uplift

We now have several thousand feet of deposition cemented together, changing it to rock, but how did we go from below sea level to over 8,500 feet in elevation? By means of the third process in Zion's evolution—uplift. This process began approximately 15 million years ago and resulted when the North American plate and the Pacific Ocean plate crashed into each other. The Pacific Ocean plate began to push and slip underneath the North American plate (a process called subduction) generating tremendous pressure against the Zion region. The Colorado Plateau, a series of fault lines, and therefore a naturally weak area, buckled under the pressure and began to lift. This process was very slow and even continues today. During the uplifting of the plateau, tremendous pressures fractured the rock formations. The many vertical fractures found throughout the Navajo sandstone are evidence of this process.

*Zion Canyon*

## Erosion

The final step of the four-step process is erosion, or the eventual destruction of Zion. As the plateau began lifting, the Virgin River began to down-cut through all the many layers of stone. Water has one desire: to reach the level of the sea. Water carves, cuts, and dissolves whatever material stands in its way in order to arrive at its final destination. The Virgin River does a very effective job in eroding Zion Canyon. Over 2 million tons of sediment or eroded rock is carried out of the canyon every year. It would take 15 dump trucks, every hour of every day, 365 days per year (the equivalent of 120,000 dump

*Angels Landing*

trucks) to carry away the same amount of material carried away each year by the Virgin River. This eroded material is transported via the Virgin River to Lake Mead, where it is deposited to someday become a new rock formation. As mentioned earlier, our earth is in a constant state of recycling itself.

## The History of Zion and Its Surrounding Areas

The earliest evidence of human life in the Zion region began about thirteen thousand years ago when the Paleo Indians inhabited the area. They were hunters and gatherers who lived off the land with whatever they could harvest. Over thousands of years Native Americans continued to occupy the area, as indicated by remnants of pueblo cliff dwellings found within the park boundaries. The Anasazi appeared to occupy this area from about A.D. 750 to 1200 when it is believed Zion was abandoned, possibly due to a change in rainfall, pressures from other peoples, or an overutilization of natural resources.

During occupation by the Anasazi culture, it is believed the tribes of the Fremont Indians also inhabited parts of the Zion region. The Fremont culture lived in small pit houses and grew corn, squash, and other vegetables. There seems to be little evidence of any connection between the two cultures. After they left around A.D. 1200, the area was not permanently occupied again until the 19th century, when small bands of the Paiute tribe began to once again occupy southwestern Utah. The Paiutes have always been considered a peaceful people and were described by early Mormon settlers as warm and helpful. During their early occupation, the Paiutes did not build permanent housing but continued to travel into favorable hunting grounds for game. The Paiute still occupy this area and are now represented in several small reservations near St. George and along the Arizona Strip.

Earliest accounts of Anglos immigrating to this area were of European descent. An expedition in 1776 by Fathers Dominguez and Escalante is the first recorded visit to Zion by Euro-Americans. At that time, the Dominguez-Escalante expedition was to locate a route from Santa Fe, New Mexico, to Monterey, California. This expedition later became the groundwork for the Spanish Trail. Approximately 50 years after the Dominguez-Escalante venture into this region, an explorer by the name of Jedidiah Smith visited the area in search of furs. Both expeditions are believed to never have seen Zion Canyon, as it was not within the routes mapped out by the explorers. Soon after the founding of Salt Lake City in 1847 by the Mormon pioneers, the Mormon Church sent scouts in search of fertile lands and locations where water was available. In 1861 many Mormon families moved south from Salt Lake City to the Zion Canyon area. St. George was founded in 1861 and dubbed "Dixie Land" because it was believed cotton could be grown and sold as the chief industry. Zion Canyon remained unexplored by Anglos through the early years of exploration of this area. It wasn't until 1858 that Paiute Indians led Nephi Johnson into the canyon where he penetrated Zion as far as the Narrows. His trek into the canyon seemed to raise little interest bamong those he told, since there was little interest in an area found deep within a canyon. In 1861, Joseph Black became interested in the possibility of farming the canyon floor, after which several farm sites were established near the current day lodge. The practice of farming and animal grazing continued until 1909, when the area was set aside as a National Monument by President Taft. The first name for the monument was Mukuntuwueap (Paiute for "Straight Canyon"). The monument was later designated Zion National Park in 1919. The name "Zion" was given to the park by Mormon settlers and refers to the Hebrew meaning of a place of safety and refuge. The Kolob section of the park was added in 1937. In Mormon theology *kolob* is a heavenly place next to God. The park was not heavily visited in the early years because the route into the park (now Highway 9) was difficult. In 1923 the Union Pacific Railroad, with a main line in Cedar City, established a roadway for automobiles, which began tourism in the park. Access to the park was limited to the West/South entrance. In 1927 the Mount Carmel Highway and Tunnel construction was started to provide access from the east.

## The Zion–Mt. Carmel Tunnel

The Zion–Mt. Carmel Tunnel and Highway were dedicated on July 4, 1930. This marked the completion of more than three years of construction costing $1.4 million. Today about one-third of park visitors enter the park via the East Entrance. This route also provides access to Bryce Canyon, the North Rim of the Grand Canyon, the Grand Staircase, Lake Powell, Capitol Reef, and many other "Canyonland Destinations." The tunnel is 1.1 mile in length and at the time of construction, the size of today's vehicles was not a consideration. The tunnel is large enough to accommodate large recreational vehicles or tour buses only when traffic is stopped and the large vehicle is allowed to travel down the center of the tunnel. A permit is required for large vehicle usage (see page 19). There are six switchbacks on the west side of the tunnel that have a gradual descent of 800 feet over 3.5

*The Zion–Mt. Carmel Tunnel*

*Pine Creek Bridge*

miles of roadway. The maximum grade is 6 percent. At the bottom of the switchbacks is the Pine Creek drainage, crossed by the Pine Creek Bridge. Notice the colors of the sandstone used to construct the bridge. An attempt was made to use every color of sandstone found within the park and the result is beautiful.

## The Building of Zion's Trail System

As you visit the park and hike the Front Country Trails, you will quickly discover the trails are paved with concrete to prevent erosion. These trails were constructed by the the CCC (Civilian Conservation Corp) during the 1930s. The trails were built using pick and shovel, and the concrete used to pave the trails was carried in backpacks as a dry mix. Pack

mules were used to carry the water for mixing concrete at the trail construction site.

## The Cable Works

From 1901 to 1926, millions of board feet of lumber were lowered from Cable Mountain to the canyon floor. In 1888, 15-year-old David Flannigan and three companions became lost while exploring the East Rim area. They wandered for several days through the great stands of ponderosa pines before coming to the edge of the great cliffs of Zion Canyon. As the group stood 1,800 feet above the canyon floor, young Flannigan decided that it would be possible to use a cable system to lower timber from the upper rim to the canyon below. Prior to this idea it had been the custom of communities along the Virgin River to haul timber by wagon from Mt. Trumbull and the Kaibab

*Remains of the cable works*

more than three years of experimenting with wire tension, braking systems, and pulleys, before they perfected the device. In 1904, with help from his father and brother, Flannigan purchased a sawmill and moved it to the East Rim. After the mill was up and running, lumber was lowered to the bottom of the canyon. By 1906, 200,000 feet of lumber had been transported by the cable system. Flannigan sold the cable works in 1907 and it continued to operate for many years. You can still see the cable works tower on the skyline of Cable Mountain from the Weeping Rock trailhead.

forest in Arizona. Flannigan thought if a cable system could be constructed, the timber would be available right here. In 1900, after trying unsuccessfully to interest anyone in his project, he undertook the project himself. The cable system consisted of 50,000 feet of telegraph wire and required the wire to be carried in bundles, on their backs, up the cliff face. Flannigan and his brothers constructed two towers to spread the wire, one at the top and one at the bottom. It took

## Zion Today

Visitors to Zion National Park experience an emotional impact when seeing the canyon for the first time. As interesting as the past is, the compelling landscape of today will exceed your expectations. This desert environment is filled with springs, streams, and seepages that support lush communities of plants and many species of animal life and provide you with spectacular scenery. You will experience hours of enjoyment, wonder, and inspiration.

*Temples and Towers of the Virgin*

# 2. Experiencing Zion National Park

## Entrance Fees

Check the park Web site for current pricing.

### Seven-Day Pass

(All passes good for seven days)

- Private vehicle
- Individual Zion Annual Pass
- National Park Pass

*Tent camper*

- Golden Eagle Passport
- Golden Age Passport
- Golden Access Passport

### Camping

Camping is available inside the park. Two campgrounds and the backcountry are camping options. Check with park officials for current pricing and regulations.

## Zion Canyon Shuttle System

In May of 2000 a shuttle system was implemented in Zion National Park. The shuttle system was necessary to enhance the visitor experience and reduce the pollution and noise impact on the Zion Canyon Scenic Drive. Prior to the shuttle it was nearly impossible to find a parking space in the main canyon and the congestion and noise disrupted the natural environment. The shuttle will operate from early April to late October each year and the 6-mile scenic drive will be closed to private vehicle traffic (except for guests stay-

## SHUTTLE FAQ

**What are the buses like?** The buses are propane powered, quiet, and airy (no air-conditioning) with large windows and skylights. Each bus is fully accessible to wheelchairs and has racks that will accommodate two bicycles. The bus and trailer will seat about 60 people.

**How often do the buses run?** The buses will start running at 6:30 AM and continue until 9:30 PM. The buses will begin each day at 15-minute intervals and increase to 6-minute intervals as need demands it.

**How much does it cost?** There is no charge for using the shuttle system. The cost of operation is included in your entrance fee.

**Are pets allowed on the bus?** Pets are not allowed on the shuttle system. Boarding for pets is available in town (see chapter 9).

**How long is the bus ride?** Round trip from the Visitor Center to the Temple of Sinawava and back again is 90 minutes. You may make the time shorter if you get off at an earlier stop and catch a bus headed back down the canyon.

**What if you have a special need?** The shuttle system was designed to reduce the congestion and im-

*Zion shuttle*

pact in Zion Canyon. Special needs do arise and arrangements can be made by contacting a ranger at the Visitor Center Information Desk.

**What about taking food containers, packs, and other personal items on the bus?** The buses do not have any storage space available. If you have personal items to carry onto the bus you must keep them with you. It is best to plan carefully when desiring to transport personal items and make them compact and as easy to handle as possible.

The shuttle system works well. The scenic drive has been restored to a wonderful and quiet place to visit.

---

ing at the lodge with a special permit that allows them to drive to the lodge only). Shuttle buses operate on two loops: In the town of Springdale (just outside the South Entrance) the shuttle stops at six locations and drops visitors off at the Zion Canyon Theatre. The Canyon loop begins at the Zion Canyon Visitor Center and stops at all trailheads, as well as Zion Lodge. Only the 6-mile scenic drive is closed to private vehicles; all other roads remain open.

### Shuttle Parking Areas

Visitors may park at designated shuttle parking areas throughout Springdale (visitors staying in Springdale can find a stop close to their place of stay) and ride the shuttle to the pedestrian entrance or enter the park by car and park at the new Visitor Center.

## Tunnel Escort Information and Fees (Large Vehicle Restrictions)

Visiting the park in a large vehicle such as an RV requires certain limitations. The Zion–Mt. Carmel Tunnel cannot handle large vehicles with normal traffic. An escort will need to be arranged in order to travel through the tunnel.

### Large Vehicle Description

Vehicles sized 7 feet 10 inches in width or 11 feet 4 inches in height or larger are considered large vehicles. Nearly all RVs, buses, trailers, fifth wheels, and some camper shells fall into the large vehicle category.

### Arranging an Escort

Visitors requiring an escort must pay a fee per vehicle

in addition to the entrance fee. Pay this fee at any entrance station before proceeding to the tunnel. The fee is good for two trips through the tunnel for the same vehicle during a seven-day period.

From October through March tunnel escorts are available from 8:00 AM to 4:30 PM daily but must be arranged in advance at the Entrance Station, Visitor Center, or by phoning 435-772-3256. Starting March 26, rangers are stationed at the tunnel from 8:00 AM to 8:00 PM. You will not be following an escort vehicle through the tunnel. Rangers will stop traffic and allow you to drive down the middle of the tunnel.

### Prohibited Vehicles

Prohibited vehicles include those larger than 13 feet 1 inch tall, semi-trucks, commercial vehicles, vehicles weighing more than 50,000 pounds, single vehicles over 40 feet long, and combined vehicles over 50 feet long, as well as bicycles and pedestrians.

## Climate and Elevation

Zion National Park is a desert environment and temperatures can be extreme. Weather conditions are typically sunny and dry; summers are warm and winters are mild.

### Average Temperatures and Precipitation

|  | High | Low | Precip. (inches) |
|---|---|---|---|
| January | 52°F | 29°F | 1.6 |
| February | 57°F | 31°F | 1.6 |
| March | 63°F | 36°F | 1.7 |
| April | 73°F | 43°F | 1.3 |
| May | 83°F | 52°F | 0.7 |
| June | 93°F | 60°F | 0.6 |
| July | 100°F | 68°F | 0.8 |
| August | 97°F | 66°F | 1.6 |
| September | 91°F | 60°F | 0.8 |
| October | 78°F | 49°F | 1.0 |
| November | 63°F | 37°F | 1.2 |
| December | 53°F | 30°F | 1.5 |

### Park Elevation

**Lowest:** 3,666 ft., Coal Pits Wash
**Highest:** 8,726 ft., Horse Ranch Mountain
**Average:** 4,000 ft., Main Canyon

## Safety and General Concerns

### Handicap Accessibility

Service dogs for the disabled are permitted on a leash anywhere in the park, including trails, buildings, shuttles, and the backcountry.

**Zion Canyon Visitor Center.** Located just inside the South Entrance to Zion National Park. Several designated parking spaces are provided with ramps leading to the main entrance. Accessible unisex restrooms, sales displays, water fountains, and telephones are also available.

**Kolob Canyon Visitor Center.** Located just off Interstate 15 at exit 40. Designated parking spaces, with a ramp leading to the building, are available. Accessible restrooms, sales displays, water fountains, and telephones are also provided.

**Zion Lodge.** Designated parking spaces and a ramp leading to the building are available. The dining room, snack bar, restrooms, and gift shop are all accessible. Two motel rooms are ADA approved. A wheelchair is available for loan.

**Zion Canyon Shuttle System.** During the busy months, use of the shuttle system is required to visit Zion Canyon. Each shuttle bus is equipped with a wheelchair lift and wheelchair seating space.

**Grotto Picnic Area.** Located up the scenic drive approximately .5 mile from Zion Lodge. Designated parking spaces available during the off season (shuttle during prime season). Picnic grounds are level but unpaved. A unisex accessible restroom is available and some tables have wheelchair extensions.

**South Campground Picnic Area.** Several tables have been set around the entrance to the south campground for picnic use. Some tables have extensions for wheelchair use. No restrooms in the immediate vicinity.

**Kolob Canyons Picnic Area.** At the end of the 5-mile scenic drive is a picnic area. There are designated parking spaces in the parking lot, and the restroom is accessible. The trail to the tables is steep and unpaved.

**South Campground.** Located just .25 mile from the south entrance. There are sites reserved for handi-

*Be careful of edges when hiking!*

capped use. The gravel-covered sites make use of wheelchairs difficult. There are extended tables, raised water spigots, and a paved trail leading to the amphitheater.

**Watchman Campground.** Located by turning right just after the south entrance and following the road around and behind the Visitor Center. There are sites reserved for handicapped use. Pavement is broken and may make wheelchair use difficult. Gravel pathways to the restroom, raised fire grills, and extended tables. A paved trail leads to the amphitheatre.

**Riverside Walk.** Accessible to wheelchairs with assistance. The 1-mile paved trail is sometimes covered with sand making travel difficult. There are some minor drop-offs with no barriers. A unisex restroom is available at the trailhead and designated parking is available.

**Lower Emerald Pools.** Accessible to wheelchairs with assistance. The .5 mile paved trail is difficult in some areas due to steep grades. There are some steep drop-offs with no barriers. Accessible restrooms are available across the street at Zion Lodge.

**Pa'rus Trail.** Accessible to wheelchairs. This 1.7-mile paved trail is also a designated bicycle path. A 10 percent grade is on the very north end of the trail. No restrooms are immediately available.

## Cliffs and Rock Falls

This is canyon country and steep cliffs and rock falls are common. Trails can have sharp drop-offs with poor footing. Be careful of edges when hiking and while using cameras or binoculars. During the winter months the trails can be snowy or ice-covered, making them slippery. Falls from trails with steep drop-offs have resulted in death.

- Stay on the trail.
- Stay back from the edges.
- Observe posted warnings.
- Parents—Watch your children!

Because of the nature of the sandstone environment, falling rocks are common. Never assume a rock is stable and will not fall. Stay away from obviously loose rocks and do not climb in areas containing loose material.

## Dehydration and High Temperatures

The low humidity and high temperatures can result in dehydration. It is much easier to become dehydrated in low humidity than in high-humidity areas. Be sure to drink plenty of water: one gallon of water per person per day. Water is available at the Visitor's Centers, campgrounds, several trailheads, and Zion Lodge. Do not drink untreated water. Flow at springs can vary and should not be trusted.

## Flash Floods

All narrow canyons are subject to flash floods. Storms that are occurring miles away can create flooding downstream. Flash floods are a real danger and can be life-threatening. During a flash flood the water rises almost instantly and can trap you in the canyon. Narrow canyons are susceptible to flooding because much of the surrounding land is bare stone that does not absorb water and acts as a channel to push waters into the drainages. Watch for these signs of possible flash flooding:

- Sudden changes in water clarity from clear to muddy or containing debris
- Rising water levels or stronger currents
- Build-up of clouds or sounds of thunder
- An increasing roar of water up-canyon
- Any deterioration in weather conditions

If you observe any of these signs, seek higher ground immediately. Do not try to outrun a flash

*A flash flood in one of Zion's canyons*

flood. Remain on high ground until conditions improve; water levels usually drop within 24 hours. If caught by flooding in an area with no high ground, try to take shelter behind a jutting fin of rock that can break the initial mass of water and debris. It may be possible to wedge yourself into a crack above water level. Climbing even a few feet may save your life.

## Hypothermia

Hypothermia occurs when the body is cooled to dangerous levels. It is the number one killer of outdoor recreationists and it usually happens without the victim's awareness. It is a hazard in narrow canyons, even in summer, because immersion in cold water is the quickest route to body heat loss. To prevent hypothermia, avoid cotton clothing (it provides no insulation when wet) and eat high-energy food (especially sugars and starches) before you are chilled. Signs of hypothermia include the following:

*Zion in winter*

- Uncontrollable shivering
- Stumbling and poor coordination
- Fatigue and weakness
- Confusion or slurred speech

*A flood in Emerald Pools*

*Zion is home to a good population of mountain lions.*

If you recognize any signs of hypothermia, stop hiking and immediately replace wet clothing with dry clothing. Warm the victim with your body or a hot drink, and take shelter from breezes. A pre-warmed sleeping bag will help prevent farther heat loss.

### Pets

As a general rule, pets are not allowed on the buses or the trails within Zion National Park. Pets must be under physical control at all times and on a leash of no longer than 6 feet. They are not allowed in the backcountry or in public buildings. There are some exceptions however: Service dogs are permitted, and pets may be walked on the Pa'rus trail. Be courteous to walkers and bicyclists. Pets left in cars can die quickly in the high heat. Do not leave your pet unattended or in a vehicle. Boarding kennels are available at La Gracias Stables and Dog Boarding (Highway 9, Rockville, UT 84763. Three minutes from the entrance to Zion. Phone: 435-772-3105, E-mail: lagracias@southernutah.com).

### Wild Animals

Part of the wonder and beauty of National Parks is the wildlife. Please respect them and keep them wild. Do not feed any wild animal. Human food is not good for them. Feeding the wildlife is illegal and can cause death or injury to the animal. Feeding wild animals may also result in injury to humans. Animals are unpredictable and can become aggressive when desiring food.

### Poisonous or Dangerous Creatures

There are several different creatures you should be aware of. Although the chances of you encountering or being injured by them is very slim, adequate precautions should be observed.

**Mountain lions (or cougars).** Zion is home to a good population of mountain lions. Typically nocturnal and very timid of humans, the odds are extremely rare that you may encounter one. In the event that you do, here is a list of dos and don'ts that should be followed:

- Avoid hiking alone, especially between dusk and dawn when lions normally do their hunting.
- Make plenty of noise while you hike so as to reduce the chances of surprising a lion.
- Always keep children in sight while hiking and within arm's reach in areas that can conceal a lion. Mountain lions seem to be drawn to children.
- Hike with a good walking stick; this can be useful in warding off a lion.
- Do not approach a lion, especially if it is feeding or with its young. Most lions will avoid confrontation. Give them a way to escape.
- Stay calm and face the lion if you come in contact. Do not run, because this may trigger the lion's instinct to attack. Try to make yourself appear larger by raising your hands.
- Pick up small children so they don't panic and run. This will also make you appear larger. Avoid bending over or crouching.
- If the lion acts aggressively, throw rocks, branches, or whatever can be obtained without turning your back or bending over.
- Fight back if attacked. Since a mountain lion usually tries to bite the head or back of the neck, try to remain standing and face the attacking animal. People have successfully fought back with rocks, sticks, or bare hands.

**Rattlesnakes.** There are several different species of rattlesnakes in the park and avoiding them is the best defense. The snakes are usually very timid and will avoid confrontations if at all possible. They will only bite you if they feel threatened.

- Always look where you are putting your feet and hands.
- Never reach into holes or dark places where a rattler may be hiding.
- Always try to stay out of tall grass if you can; watch where you are stepping if you can't.
- Always gather firewood during the daytime; rattlers are more active at night.
- Always wear thick shoes in snake country.
- Never pick up a snake, even if it looks dead. It might not be dead, but just pretending to be.
- Never make quick moves if you see a rattlesnake or hear its rattle. Back up slowly—but be sure you don't back into another snake.

If bitten, try to remember the following:

- Don't panic! Remember what the snake looked like and look to make sure the fangs actually broke the skin.
- Get a doctor as soon as possible, but send somebody else to do it, if possible. If you run, your heart will pump faster and the poison will spread faster.
- Never try to treat a snakebite by yourself, unless there is no chance of getting to a doctor.

**Scorpions.** Most scorpion stings from the species found in Zion are not fatal. All stings should be taken seriously and medical attention obtained if you are stung. Scorpions are most common at night and will hide under rocks, limbs, or in crevices. If camping outside you should always check clothing before dressing and check your sleeping gear before lying down.

**Black widow spider.** The black widow spider is common in Zion and can be found just about anywhere. Watch for the spider in dark, shaded areas such as crevices, rodent burrows, and rock and debris piles. Most widow bites are not fatal but medical attention should be sought.

**Brown recluse spider.** This spider seems to prefer the dry, nonirrigated areas. They can be found under logs, rocks, debris, and in packrat nests. The bite will

*The Western rattlesnake, a resident of Zion*

*Ron and the Travel Channel*

cause flu-like symptoms within two to eight hours. If bitten, seek medical attention immediately.

**Bees, wasps, ants, and other insects.** Other insects may bite you and individual reactions may differ. If you have any reaction to a bite, you should seek medical attention immediately.

### Emergencies and Medical Services

For 24-hour emergency response, call 435-772-3322 or 911. Zion Canyon Medical Clinic is in Springdale, call for hours, 435-772-3226. The nearest hospitals are in St. George, Cedar City, and Kanab.

## Ranger Programs and Activities

### Junior Ranger Program

A Junior Ranger Program is offered daily throughout the summer season for kids ages 6–12. The programs offer supervised educational programs where the kids can become a "Junior Ranger" and earn several different awards based on participation.

### Ranger Programs

Ranger Programs are offered daily throughout the summer season. Programs being offered are posted at the Visitor Center and other areas throughout the park. Limited programs are available during the fall, winter, and early spring.

**Guided Hikes.** Guided nature walks or hikes are offered daily by interpretive park rangers.

**Ranger-Guided Shuttle Tours.** During the months of shuttle operation, rangers will provide guided shuttle tours of the main canyon.

**Museum, Visitor Center, or Lodge Talks.** Short interpretive talks are offered daily at the museum, Visitor Center, or at Zion Lodge.

**Evening Programs.** Ranger programs are offered nightly at the campground amphitheatres or Zion Lodge.

*Ranger Ron leading a guided hike*

*Orderville Canyon*

# 3. Main Canyon Trip Planner

Zion National Park offers a wide variety of activities: Ranger Programs, Guided Hikes, Junior Ranger Program for kids, or self-exploration. Whether you are visiting for just a short time or you have elected to stay for a while, the following suggestions and descriptions will help you make the best use of your time.

## One-Day Visit

Stop by the Visitor Center and enjoy the new facility and outdoor displays. Board the shuttle (no need to be in a hurry—they leave every few minutes all day long) and take a ride up through the 6-mile scenic drive. Round-trip riding time is 90 minutes. Visit the lodge for lunch or visit the gift shop. Horseback riding is available from the lodge and consists of one-hour or three-hour rides. If you would to hike some short trails, the following are suggested (see the trail descriptions to help you decide):

- **The Riverside Walk**
  Easy
  2 miles—about one hour round-trip
- **The Weeping Rock Trail**
  Easy
  .5 mile—about 30 minutes round-trip
- **The Emerald Pools Trail**
  Easy
  1–2.5 miles—one to two hours round-trip

*A view from Canyon Overlook*

Go to a Ranger Program—several are offered daily (see Ranger Programs, page 26).

If you elect to take a driving tour the following routes are suggested:

- **The Zion–Mt. Carmel Highway**
  (13 miles from the south to the east entrances)
- **The Kolob Terrace Road**
  (23 miles from Virgin City turnoff)
- **The Kolob Canyons Scenic Drive**
  (5-mile scenic drive)

## Two-Day Visit

Continue with exploring the previous trails or consider hiking some of the other trails found in the canyon:

- **The Pa'rus Trail**
  Easy
  5 miles—two hours round-trip
- **The Watchman Trail**
  Moderate
  2 miles—1.5 hours round-trip
- **The Canyon Overlook**
  Moderate
  1 mile—one hour round-trip
- **Hidden Canyon Trail**
  Moderate
  2 miles—three hours round-trip
- **The Angels Landing**
  Strenuous
  5 miles—3.5 hours round-trip
- **The Observation Point**
  Strenuous
  8 miles—five hours round-trip
- **The Narrows**
  (from Riverside to Orderville area)
  Strenuous
  6 or more miles—five hours round-trip

Explore the area (see chapter 9, page 79), attend another Ranger Program, take a scenic drive, go bicycling (see chapter 8, page 78), or just relax.

## Three-Day (or More) Visit

Explore the region; venture out for the day and be back in time for a relaxing evening (see chapter 9, page 79). Continue to explore the previous trails or consider doing a trip into the backcountry for an overnighter (See chapter 5, "Backcountry Trip Planner"). However you choose to spend your time in Zion National Park, the visit will be rewarding and memorable.

# 4. Main Canyon Trail Descriptions

## Zion Canyon

Zion Canyon offers a wide variety of walks or hikes with easy access to the trailheads. Use the following trail guide to help you in choosing a hike that may be appropriate for you. The trails range from easy and flat to strenuous and steep, all offering views, formations, and an experience you will never forget.

### The Riverside Walk

**Difficulty:** Easy
**Length:** 2 miles round-trip
**Average Time:** One hour
**Ascent:** 69 ft.
**Drop-offs:** Minor
**Sun Exposure:** Shaded
**Trail Type:** Paved
**Restrooms:** Yes

The Riverside Walk begins at the Temple of Sinawava and is considered the "Gateway to the Narrows." The trail was constructed in 1925 and then resurveyed and realigned in 1929. At that time the rock retaining walls were built and the entire trail widened to 5 feet. In 1930 water from a spring high on the face of the west wall at the Temple of Sinawava was piped down and across the river. Two drinking fountains were installed, one of which remains today. On August 1st, 1968 a rock slide from the east wall buried 250 feet of the trail near its end under 23 feet of debris. Several park visitors were trapped at the far end and bridging across the river had to be improvised to rescue them. Reconstruction over the top of the rubble pile was completed in 1970. The trail follows the Virgin River below the tall vertical cliffs. Along the trail you will see hanging gardens in the sandstone cliffs and water seepages that provide a lush and cool environment for wildflowers such as golden columbine, blue shooting stars, cliff columbine, orange monkeyflower, and maidenhair fern. The towering cliffs above will instill you with feelings of wonder and awe. The trail has a desert swamp area and many forms of plant life and trees. Adorning the walk are wild grapes and many different flowers. There are trailside exhibits and benches where you can rest. You may also find many

*Let's hike!*

species of wild animals such as mule deer, squirrels, and possibly the Zion snail. Winter closures are possible due to falling ice.

### Weeping Rock Trail

**Difficulty:** Easy
**Length:** .5 mile round-trip
**Average Time:** 30 minutes
**Ascent:** 98 ft.
**Drop-offs:** Minor
**Sun Exposure:** Shaded
**Trail Type:** Paved
**Restrooms:** Yes

The Weeping Rock Trail is a short but somewhat steep ascent to a rock alcove with dripping water. Along the paved trail you will find interpretive signs introducing you to the plant life found in this area. The alcove has hanging gardens that are adorned with wildflowers such as golden columbine, blue shooting stars, cliff columbine, orange monkeyflower, and maidenhair fern. The water you see dripping from this area is somewhere between 1,000 and 4,000 years old. It takes that long to filter down through the sandstone. The trail is abundant with plant life, birds, and other wild animals. Winter closures are possible due to ice.

# Emerald Pools Trail System

(From Zion Lodge) The Emerald Pools Trail System was constructed in 1925. In 1926, two suspension bridges were put in (one at the grotto and the other at the lodge). Sometime after 1984 the suspension bridges were replaced with steel arch bridges. The Emerald Pools are so named because of the emerald-green algae growing in them.

## Lower Emerald Pools

**Difficulty:** Easy
**Length:** 1.2 miles round-trip
**Average Time:** One hour
**Ascent:** 69 ft.
**Drop-offs:** Minor
**Sun Exposure:** Shaded
**Trail Type:** Paved
**Restrooms:** At Zion Lodge

The Lower Emerald Pools trail begins across the street from the Zion Lodge. The trail is lined with oak, pinyon, juniper, and cottonwood trees. You will travel .6 miles to the base of the Emerald Pools Waterfalls that fall 110 feet to the lower pools. This trail allows you to walk behind the waterfalls and next to the rock cliffs that are adorned with hanging gardens of wildflowers such as golden columbine, blue shooting stars, cliff columbine, orange monkeyflower, and maidenhair fern. The pools are covered in rich emerald green moss (hence the name) and provide a place of peace and serenity. Wild animals may be seen along the trail; watch especially for the Zion Canyon tree frog. Winter closures possible due to ice.

## Middle Emerald Pools

**Difficulty:** Moderate
**Length:** 2 miles round-trip

**Average Time:** Two hours
**Ascent:** 150 ft.
**Drop-offs:** Long
**Sun Exposure:** Thru mid-afternoon
**Trail Type:** Unpaved, sand
**Restrooms:** At Zion Lodge

The Middle Emerald Pools trail begins across the street from the Zion Lodge and will ascend up a moderately steep trail that walks along the bench through pinyon and juniper trees. The trail leads you to the middle pools that are the top of the waterfalls to the lower pools. This trail requires that you cross the streams and may be difficult during high-water conditions. The views from the cliff edge of the canyon and cliffs are beautiful. Watch for animals, birds, and wildflowers along the trail. Winter closures possible due to ice and snow.

## Upper Emerald Pools

**Difficulty:** Moderate
**Length:** .6 miles round-trip
**Average Time:** One hour
**Ascent:** 200 ft.
**Drop-offs:** Minor
**Sun Exposure:** Thru mid-afternoon
**Trail Condition:** Sandy and rocky
**Restrooms:** None

The Upper Emerald Pools trail begins at the Middle Pools. The trail will ascend 200 feet to the base of the cliff, where the Emerald Pools water source begins from rock seepage. Your trail takes you through the pinyon and juniper trees. The pool is located at the base of the cliffs and is the largest of the pools. During the winter months or high-water times a waterfall is present that falls nearly 800 feet to the pool. Watch for animals, birds, and wildflowers along this trail. Winter closures possible.

## Kayenta Trail

**Difficulty:** Moderate
**Length:** 2 miles round-trip
**Average Time:** Two hours
**Ascent:** 150 ft.
**Drop-offs:** Long
**Sun Exposure:** Thru mid-afternoon
**Trail Type:** Unpaved, sand/rocky
**Restrooms:** Yes, at trailhead (Grotto)

The Kayenta Trail begins at the Grotto Picnic Area and travels along the bench after ascending 150 feet. Receiving its name from the Kayenta Formation, which the trail traverses, the trail passes through pinyon and juniper forests and is host to many wildflowers during the spring. This trail is considered the "backdoor" approach to the Emerald Pools area. The views from this trail of the Great White Throne, Red Arch Mountain, and the Virgin River are spectacular. Watch for wild animals, birds, and flowers along this route. Using this trail in conjunction with the Emerald Pools trails will provide a loop from the lodge and back again. Winter closures possible.

## Grotto Trail

**Difficulty:** Easy
**Length:** .5 mile
**Average Time:** 20 minutes
**Ascent:** 20 ft.
**Drop-offs:** Minor
**Sun Exposure:** Shaded
**Trail Type:** Unpaved, sand
**Restrooms:** Yes, grotto/lodge

The Grotto Trail is considered a connector trail between the lodge and Grotto Picnic Area. The trail travels through the cottonwood trees and parallels the canyon road. Wild animals, birds, and flowers may be seen from this trail.

## Hidden Canyon Trail

**Difficulty:** Moderate
**Length:** 2 miles round-trip
**Average Time:** Three hours
**Ascent:** 850 ft.
**Drop-offs:** Long
**Sun Exposure:** Full sun
**Trail Type:** Paved, narrow
**Restrooms:** Yes, at trailhead

The Hidden Canyon Trail was constructed in 1928 after Park Rangers explored the area in 1927 while searching for W. H. Evans, the first man to climb the Great White Throne. He fell while descending and was critically injured. The trail along the sheer cliff edge was blasted out of the solid rock for hikers wanting to enter the hidden canyon area. The Hidden Canyon Trail begins at the Weeping Rock trailhead and travels up switchbacks to a narrow side canyon.

The first portion of switchbacks is steep but wide. The last section of trail before entering the narrow slot canyon is very narrow with steep, long drop-offs on one side of the trail. This trail is not recommended for people fearful of heights. There are chains to hold on to as you cross the narrow section. Once you have reached the hidden canyon you can hike back into the canyon for about .6 mile before being stopped by boulders. The canyon trail offers beautiful views of the main canyon and of Angels Landing. Winter closures possible. As with all narrow canyons, this one should be avoided during threat of rain.

## Angels Landing Trail

**Difficulty:** Strenuous
**Length:** 5 miles round-trip
**Average Time:** Four hours
**Ascent:** 1488 ft.
**Drop-offs:** Long
**Sun Exposure:** Full Sun
**Trail Type:** Paved/sandstone
**Restrooms:** Yes, trailhead/grotto

Angels Landing got its name from Reverend Fisher in 1916 when it was stated that only angels could land

## Map Key

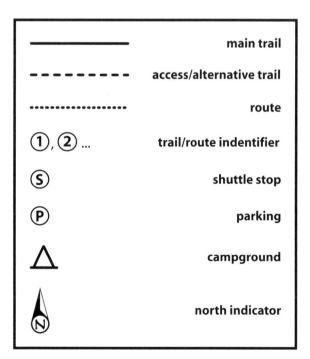

| | |
|---|---|
| ———————— | **main trail** |
| – – – – – – – – | **access/alternative trail** |
| ·················· | **route** |
| ①, ② ... | **trail/route indentifier** |
| Ⓢ | **shuttle stop** |
| Ⓟ | **parking** |
| △ | **campground** |
| Ⓝ | **north indicator** |

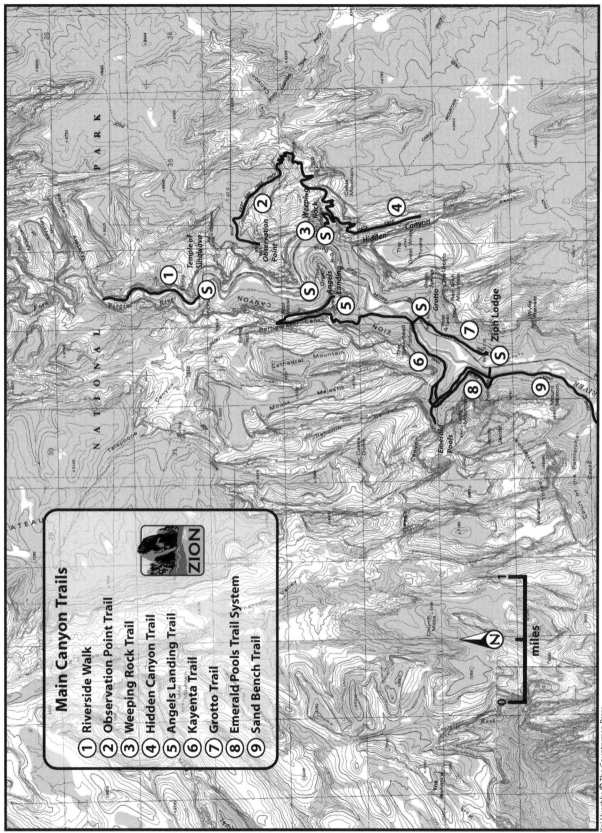

## Main Canyon Trails

1. Riverside Walk
2. Observation Point Trail
3. Weeping Rock Trail
4. Hidden Canyon Trail
5. Angels Landing Trail
6. Kayenta Trail
7. Grotto Trail
8. Emerald Pools Trail System
9. Sand Bench Trail

ZION

miles

0                    1

Kai Huschke © The Countryman Press

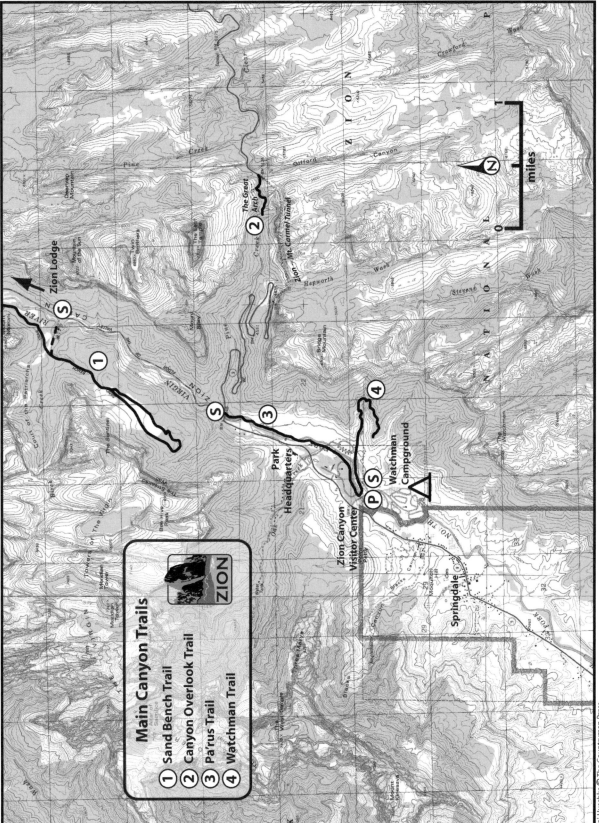

Main Canyon Trails

1 Sand Bench Trail
2 Canyon Overlook Trail
3 Pa'rus Trail
4 Watchman Trail

Kai Huschke © The Countryman Press

*Hop Valley*

backs you will enter Refrigerator Canyon, where you will get a reprieve from the sun. This narrow canyon will continue for about .5 mile,, where you then begin a steep ascent up switchbacks called "Walter's Wiggles." The very steep switchbacks are an engineering marvel and worth the hike just to see them. Once at the top of the wiggles you will be at Scout Lookout, the base of Angels Landing. The trail is paved to this point. From the base of Angels Landing you will ascend up a sandstone trail for .5 mile to the top of the landing. This last .5 mile is a very narrow ridge on a very narrow trail with drop-offs on both sides of the trail that are more than 1,200 feet straight down. This hike is not recommended for people fearful of heights. Angels Landing is a hike of spectacular scenery and will be one that you will not soon forget. Highly recommended!

## Observation Point Trail

**Difficulty:** Strenuous
**Length:** 8 miles round-trip
**Average Time:** Five hours
**Ascent:** 2148 ft.
**Drop-offs:** Long
**Sun Exposure:** Full sun
**Trail Type:** Paved/sand
**Restrooms:** Yes, at trailhead

This trail was constructed in 1925 but the route was definitely used in early years as passage to the East Rim by Paiutes. Whether the Anasazi people before them used the same trail is open to conjecture, but some 20 steps cut into the sheer rock face above the Weeping Rock parking lot are still visible today. The Observation Point Trail begins at Weeping Rock and ascends switchbacks to the East Mesa Trail. This hike route will take you up the side of Cable Mountain and into Echo Canyon. The trail intersects with the East Rim, Cable Mountain, and Deertrap Mountain trails. This route offers a large diversity in plant life as you begin climbing through pinyon and juniper and work your way into the ponderosa pines. The full length of the trail offers you slick rock formations and spectacular views of the canyon. The trail ends at an overlook giving you a birds-eye view of the Great White Throne, Cable Mountain, the West Rim, and Angels Landing. This trail can be hazardous during winter conditions.

on it. Angels Landing is accessed via the West Rim Trail. The West Rim Trail was constructed in 1925 by dynamiting into the face of the cliff leading to Refrigerator Canyon. By the spring of 1926 Walter's Wiggles had been built and the new trail was complete to Scout Lookout. Crown Prince Gustavus and Princess Louise of Sweden dedicated the trail on July 11, 1926. The trail was originally named the "Royal Trail" in their honor. The trail to Angels Landing from Scout Lookout was later constructed and 500 feet of pipe railing was installed for the more timid hiker along the more dangerous sections. The Angels Landing Trail starts at the Grotto Picnic Area, where you cross the river bridge and begin your hike up the West Rim Trail. The trail travels through the pinyon/juniper forest for about .5 mile before starting a steep ascent up switchbacks. After the first set of switch-

## Sand Bench Trail

**Difficulty:** Moderate
**Length:** 3.6 miles round-trip
**Average Time:** Three hours
**Ascent:** 500 ft.
**Drop-offs:** Minor
**Sun Exposure:** Shaded
**Trail Type:** Sand
**Restrooms:** Yes, Zion Lodge

The earliest pioneers used the Sand Bench Trail as a means of getting up the canyon because the river valley was so often impassable due to frequent flooding. The Sand Bench Trail will lead you along the Virgin River on the cliff bench. The loop trail passes an ancient landslide and below the streaked wall. There are good views of the Three Patriarchs and the lower canyon. You will be walking through many different species of trees such as the Fremont Cottonwood, pinyon pine, and junipers. Watch for wild turkeys in this area, as well as other wildlife. Note: This trail is used by the horseback riders during summer months and is better used as a winter hike.

## The Watchman Trail

**Difficulty:** Moderate
**Length:** 2 miles round-trip
**Average Time:** Two hours
**Ascent:** 368 ft.
**Drop-offs:** Minor
**Sun Exposure:** Full sun
**Trail Type:** Sand/rocks
**Restrooms:** No

The Watchman Trail, constructed in 1934, was originally cut as a passage into Parunuweap Canyon but the difficulties with rockslides made it impossible to reach the destination. It was even called the Parunuweap Trail, but the name has since changed to Watchman Trail and a spur was built out to the present viewpoint. This trail begins east of the Visitor Center, beyond the transportation-building turnoff. The trail climbs through the lower desert region and onto a plateau. This area is abundant with wildflowers and offers a variety of wildlife. From the plateau you have great views of the Watchman, Temples of the Virgin, Oak Creek Canyon, and the town of Spring-

dale. This trail can be muddy during rain or winter months but is an excellent place to observe sunset.

## Canyon Overlook Trail

**Difficulty:** Moderate
**Length:** 1 mile round-trip
**Average** Time: One hour
**Ascent:** 163 ft.
**Drop-offs:** Long
**Sun Exposure:** Full sun
**Trail Condition:** Sandstone
**Restrooms:** Yes, at trailhead

The Canyon Overlook Trail was constructed in 1932. This trail offers interpretive leaflets at the trailhead and is a great source of information as you walk this trail. The trail environment is much different than those of the main canyon; the plants and animals are adapted to living in the rock and sand habitat. As you ascend the trail, look to your left and you will see Pine Creek Canyon, dubbed "Fat Mans Peril" because of the very narrow slot cut through the sandstone. The trail will take you to a rock alcove overhang that is lush with maidenhair fern. As you reach the end of the trail, you will be on the top of the Great Arch of Zion observed from the switchbacks as you approach the tunnel. The views are spectacular of the West Temple, East Temple, Towers of the Virgin, and the Streaked Wall. As you hike the trail, keep your eyes on the south side of the canyons and you might be able to see the Desert Bighorn sheep. The sheep are usually high on the cliffs and difficult to see. On the return trip, look for a rock formation along the trail that resembles a turtle. This hike is an excellent place to observe a sunrise.

## Pa'rus Trail

**Difficulty:** Easy
**Length:** 3.5 miles round-trip
**Average Time:** 1.5 hours
**Ascent:** 50 ft.
**Drop-offs:** None
**Sun Exposure:** Full sun/shaded
**Trail Type:** Paved
**Restrooms:** South Campground

The Pa'rus Trail was constructed in 1995 as part of the impending shuttle transportation system to allow pedestrian and bicycle traffic a safe route to the main

*Checkerboard Mesa*

canyon. The Pa'rus Trail is a relatively flat trail that follows the Virgin River from the South Campground to the Canyon Junction. The word *pa'rus* comes from the Paiute Indian word meaning "tumbling water." Great views of the lower canyon are available along this trail and it's a good place for bird watching. This trail is the only trail in Zion that allows you to ride a bicycle or walk your dog. The plant life is diverse and wildlife can be seen from just about anywhere on the trail. This trail is a great way to access the main canyon by foot or bicycle.

# Scenic Viewpoints

### The Court of the Patriarchs

The Court of the Patriarchs is one of the shuttle stops and is located 2.2 miles up the main canyon drive. An easy walk up a 50-yard trail to the viewpoint offers views of the Court of the Patriarchs, the Streaked Wall, the Sentinel, Angels Landing, Mt. Moroni, the Spearhead, Mountain of the Sun, and the Twin Brothers. (See chapter 13 for cliff name origins.)

### Big Bend

This area is found about .25 mile beyond the Weeping Rock Trailhead and is one of the shuttle stops. The area offers views of the Virgin River, the Great White Throne, Cable Mountain, Angels Landing, and Organ. This is also a great place to view mountain climbers during the spring and fall months (climbing during the summer months is just too hot). Also visible from this area is the only remnant of an Anasazi granary, which can be seen in the rock alcove near Weeping Rock. (See chapter 13 for name origins.)

### Checkerboard Mesa

This area is found near the east entrance and offers a great view of Checkerboard Mesa, a prominent feature in the park with patterns in the sandstone that look like a checkerboard. Views of Quilt Mesa, the White Cliffs, and other prominent sandstone formations are also visible.

*Coalpits Wash*

# 5. Backcountry Trip Planner

Zion National Park offers some of the greatest backcountry opportunities anywhere. The spectacular scenery will afford the visitor memories of a lifetime.

## Hiking the Backcountry

Permits are required for all overnight backpacking, all through-hikes of rivers and tributaries, all climbing bivouacs, and all canyons requiring the use of technical gear or ropes. Permits may be obtained from the Backcountry Office located in each of the Visitor's Centers. For current pricing and other regulations, call the Backcountry Office at 435-772-0170.

### Group Size

All backcountry areas are limited to group sizes of no more than 12 people. The park service is very strict about this, so you should plan accordingly.

### Camping Areas

You must camp in designated campsites or areas and out of sight and sound of the trails. Camp at least .25 mile from springs. If camping in narrow canyons, be aware of the potential for flash flooding and camp above high-water marks.

## Plan Carefully

Trips into the backcountry require advance planning. Even short trips need to be planned for. The weather conditions can be extreme hot in the summer and cold in the winter. Always check weather conditions prior to the hike and visit with rangers for any special precautions. Be prepared to hike the backcountry by having a preplanned route, plenty of water, food, and

*Tiger salamander*

other needed equipment. Whether you are hiking, climbing, or driving, your safety depends on your own good judgment. Having an accident is a very poor way of shortening your vacation.

## Hiking with Minimum Impact

When hiking within Zion National Park, please be sensitive to the fragile environment that makes this area so special. When hiking, stay on trails when possible and avoid trampling vegetation or taking short-cuts. When making campsite selections, always camp out of sight of the trails, stay at least .25 mile from water sources (when possible), do not make campsite improvements such as constructing benches, tables, etc.—if you carry it in, carry it out. Human waste must be buried at least .25 mile from any water source. Dig a hole 8 inches deep and cover all waste when finished; however do not bury toilet paper, carry it out. Use zippered plastic pouches for waste receptacles. All water should be filtered, treated, or boiled before drinking. When using water to bathe, wash dishes, or clean camping supplies, use only biodegradable soap and carry water at least .25 mile from water source. Open fires are not allowed anywhere in the backcountry of Zion National Park.

*The rocks of Coalpits Wash*

# 6. Backcountry Trail Descriptions

## Virgin River Drainage

### The Zion Narrows

**Difficulty:** Strenuous

This is one of the most popular hikes in Zion Canyon. The Virgin River has carved a narrow, slot canyon through the Navajo sandstone. The hike is 16 miles long with canyon walls over 2,000 feet high. At some points the canyon walls are only 20 feet apart. This is a hike that is unforgettable. This hike should never be underestimated; it can be taxing, dangerous, and cold. The hike requires you to hike in the Virgin River. The water can be anywhere from ankle deep to waist deep, with some areas requiring you to swim. The river is swift, cold, and you are walking on boulders that are slippery. Proper equipment is essential in making this hike. The following are recommended:

- Good, sturdy hiking boots
- A walking stick
- Plenty of water
- First-aid kit
- Waterproof containers (for cameras, etc.)
- Extra food
- Flashlight
- Extra warm clothes
- Trash bags for packing out trash
- Sunscreen, sunglasses, hat

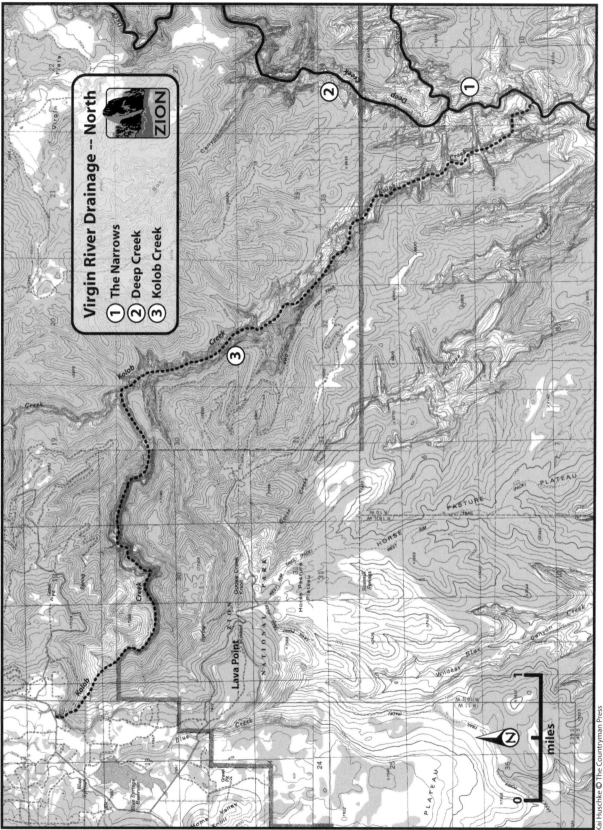

Virgin River Drainage -- North

ZION

1 The Narrows
2 Deep Creek
3 Kolob Creek

Kai Huschke © The Countryman Press

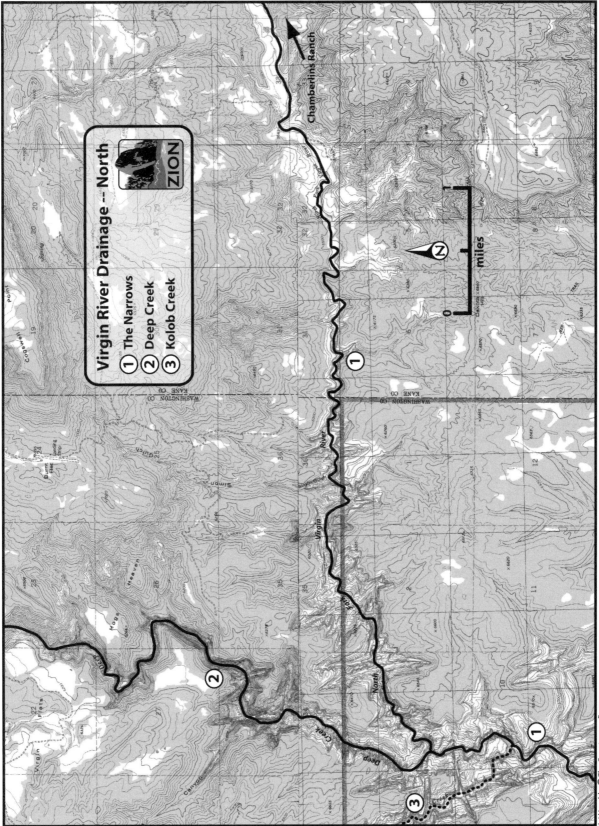

Virgin River Drainage -- North

ZION

1 The Narrows
2 Deep Creek
3 Kolob Creek

Kai Huschke © The Countryman Press

# When to Hike the Narrows

Typically the best months for hiking the Narrows are June, July, and September. However, hiking can be done at any time with proper planning and equipment. Hiking the Narrows during the winter requires cold-weather gear and a dry suit. Warning: Hiking the Narrows can be hazardous at any time and is subject to flash flooding. Late July and August are particularly prone to flooding. Always check with the Visitor Center for current weather and hazard concerns.

# Three Ways to Hike the Narrows

### Day Hike from the Bottom and Back
(No Permit Required)

This is the most common way to see the Narrows. The hike begins at the temple of Sinawava. Take the Riverside Walk for 1 mile back to the river's edge; from that point you will be required to enter the water. The hike will traverse through water and on to shoreline for 2 miles. Located about .25 mile upstream is Mystery Falls, a waterfall on the right-hand side of the canyon. Each bend in the river will bring new scenery and adventure. This hike has no formal destination and can be as short or long as you would like. To reach the "narrowest" part of the canyon (like you see in the pictures) will take about two hours of hiking time from the end of the Riverside Walk. You will know when you have reached this area because you'll see Orderville Canyon on the right and there is no longer any shoreline. "Big Springs" is the narrowest part of the canyon and will take an additional two hours (traveling beyond Big Springs is prohibited). Orderville Canyon enters the canyon from the right and is also a great place to explore.

### Day Hike from the Top Down
(Permit Required)

This is probably the most difficult way to hike the narrows. The hike is 16 miles in length and will take at least 12 hours. The trailhead is at Chamberlain's Ranch, a 1.5-hour drive from the Visitor Center, and will require finding transportation or having two vehicles. Transportation is available and arrangements should be made before obtaining a permit.

### Overnight Hike from the Top Down
(Permit Required)

This is the best way to enjoy the 16-mile hike of the Narrows. You can take your time and experience the canyon. There are campsites located above the watermark along the route. Only one-night stays are allowed.

Campsites are assigned on a first-come, first-serve basis. Permits may be obtained the day before or on the day of the hike.

### Directions to Chamberlain's Ranch

Chamberlain's Ranch is a 1.5-hour drive from the Visitor Center. The route has both paved and dirt roads. The dirt roads can be impassable during wet weather. From the east entrance, drive 2.5 miles on Highway 9 to the North Fork Road, turn left, and travel 18 miles to a wooden bridge. Turn left past the bridge and drive .25 mile to the gate. Please close the gate behind you. Drive .5 mile farther and park just before the road crosses the river. The hike begins across the river and follows the road for about 3 miles. Enter the river at the end of the road.

# Orderville Canyon

(For more information about this section of the Narrows, see the canyoneering route description on page 63.)

# Deep Creek

**Difficulty:** Strenuous
**Length:** 22.6 miles one way
**Average Time:** Allow 3 days
**Approx. Elevation:** 5,000 ft.
**Drop-offs:** Long
**Sun Exposure:** Full sun/shaded
**Trail Type:** Sand/rock/stream
**Water Source:** Stream

This hike is along one of the major tributaries of the Virgin River and will require hiking a great deal of the time in the water. The travel time is slow because of heavy brush and slick boulders. The area hosts a variety of plant and animal life with large lava flows, beautiful cliff formations, and scenic water cascades. To access this hike you must go to Cedar City and take Highway 14 east until you find Cedar Canyon Campground, continue past there until you locate Webster Flat Road on the right (approximately 15 miles from Cedar City). Take Webster Flat Road,

*Orderville Canyon*

downstream from the confluence by walking on the right side of the stream, high on the ridge until you find a pathway back down to the stream. Several campsites are located near the O'Neil Gulch/Deep Creek confluence. From this point forward you will be hiking through Gambel oaks and on rolling hills. The hike continues to follow the stream for a short distance and then you will follow an animal trail to the bench on the right side of the stream. Follow the bench through the oak for about 1 mile, where it will return to the stream. After reaching the streams you will be hiking downstream through heavy brush until you reach Corral Canyon. From there continue downstream past the lava flows, past Crystal Creek, and finally into the Deep Creek Narrows. Once inside the Narrows, you will find some campsites suitable for good-weather camping. Continue downstream, where you will encounter slippery boulders and some pools. This portion of the hike is very slow going. This beautiful narrow canyon will be worth the time it takes to make it down through here. The Deep Creek Narrows are about 6 miles in length before reaching the Virgin River Confluence. From the confluence to the Temple of Sinawava is approximately 8 miles. Campsites 2 through 12 are from this point down. Consider spending your second night here. This area is subject to flash flooding and is very dangerous during inclement weather. Check with the Backcountry Office for current weather conditions, required permits, and other precautions before attempting this hike.

# East Rim Hikes
## East Entrance to Weeping Rock

(See map on page 46)
**Difficulty:** Moderate
**Length:** 10.6 miles one-way
**Average Time:** Seven hours
**Approx. Elevation:** 6,500 ft.
**Drop-offs:** Long
**Sun Exposure:** Full sun/shaded
**Trail Type:** Sand/rocks/paved
**Restrooms:** None
**Water Source:** Stave Springs

The East Rim Trail was constructed in 1926. Prior to that the trail was known as the old Winder Stock Trail. The East Rim Trail is a mountainous trail leav-

where you will leave the Dixie National Forest boundary, and continue down the main roadway until you reach a valley with a stream meandering through it. This area is Fife Creek, and you will begin your hike in the culvert. Work your way down between the Lava Fields and Aspen Trees on the left-hand side of the creek. Continue down the path, where you will need to climb two fences and will find a valley to the left. Continue downstream to the log fence, cross it, and stay on the right side of the stream. About 75 yards downstream look for the small drainage entering from the right, go up this drainage, and locate a path that will take you uphill and that connects with an old dirt road. Follow the dirt road past Big Spring to where the road climbs the west side of the canyon. Continue on the road just past Big Spring until you locate a trail on the left. Follow the trail to the left until you cross a fence and locate the confluence of Deep Creek and Fife Creek. This is a nice area to camp. Continue

ing from the east entrance area of the Park. The trail will take you through forested areas consisting of pinyon, juniper, and ponderosa pines. The terrain is rolling and will have some short, steep descents until you reach the canyon rim. The first 2 miles of the hike will afford you great views of the Checkerboard Mesa, Jolley Gulch, and the White Cliffs area. From the canyon rim to the canyon floor the trail is steep, with long drop-offs. The wildflowers are plentiful during the spring and summer months. Wildlife may be spotted from anywhere along the trail. Once on the rim of the canyon, you will experience spectacular views of the main canyon and west rim. The area was logged during the early settlement years and the timber was lowered into the canyon via the Cable Works. This area can be impassable during winter months due to snow and muddy conditions.

## East Entrance to Cable Mountain

(See map on page 46)
**Difficulty:** Moderate
**Length:** 17 miles round-trip
**Average time:** 10 hours
**Approx. Elevation:** 6,500 ft.
**Drop-offs:** Long at canyon rim
**Sun Exposure:** Full sun/shaded
**Trail Type:** Sand/rocks
**Restrooms:** None
**Water Source:** Stave Springs

The Cable Mountain Trail was constructed in 1900 as a wagon trail to haul lumber from a sawmill at Stave Springs to the Cable Works at the Crest of Cable Mountain. This trail will be mountainous terrain through pinyon, juniper, and ponderosa pines. The hike will take you along the East Rim Trail to Stave Springs, where you will branch off and follow the Cable Mountain Trail to the canyon rim. From the canyon rim you will see the historic Cable Works and spectacular views of Zion Canyon and the West Rim. Open camping is available in this area; check with the Backcountry Office for information and required permits. This area may be impassable during the winter months due to snow and muddy conditions.

## East Entrance to Deertrap Mountain

(See map on page 46)
**Difficulty:** Moderate
**Length:** 17.6 mi round-trip
**Average Time:** 10.5 hours
**Approx. Elevation:** 6,500 ft.
**Drop-offs:** Long at canyon rim
**Sun Exposure:** Full sun/shaded
**Trail Type:** Sand/rocks
**Restrooms:** None
**Water Source:** Stave Springs

The Deertrap Mountain Trail was constructed in the early 1900s as a wagon trail for harvesting lumber. This trail will branch off of the East Rim trail and continue to Deertrap Mountain. This trail offers spectacular views of the canyon from the rim and is abundant with wildlife and wildflowers. Camping is allowed in this area, check with the Backcountry Office for information and required permits. This area may be impassable during the winter months due to snow and muddy conditions.

# East Side Hikes
## Checkerboard Mesa Drainage to the Rim of Parunuweap Canyon

**Difficulty:** Moderate
**Length:** 6 miles round-trip
**Average Time:** Four hours
**Approx. Elevation:** 6,000 ft.
**Drop-offs:** Minor
**Sun Exposure:** Shaded/full sun
**Trail Type:** Rock/sand
**Restrooms:** None
**Water Source:** None

Beginning at the large pullout in the mouth of the Checkerboard Mesa Drainage (between Checkerboard Mesa and Quilt Mesa, about .25 mile before the Checkerboard Mesa Viewpoint) follow the drainage east into the canyon. This hike will take you into a narrow slot canyon, with ponderosa pines, pinyons, junipers, and a diverse collection of plant life. A favorite place for birds and other wildlife, the cliff formations are spectacular. Staying in the bottom of the drainage, follow the narrow canyon for about 1 mile to the saddle. Look for the path of use taking you up and over the saddle; this area is very steep and difficult hiking until you have reached the widened canyon on the opposite side. Once you have negotiated the saddle, continue to follow the drainage, staying left, where you can avoid walking in the sand and walk on the sandstone. The drainage will eventually reach Parunuweap Canyon (East Fork of the Virgin River). Once on the canyon rim, turn north and follow the canyon edge for about .25 mile to an overlook of the waterfalls deep in the canyon. The views of the canyon are beautiful with cliffs dropping over 1,000 feet. Note: Parunuweap Canyon is closed to exploration. Do not attempt an excursion to the bottom. For the return trip, and to avoid getting lost, it is best to retrace your route.

## Cave Canyon—East Fork

**Difficulty:** Moderate
**Length:** 1.5 miles one way
**Average Time:** Three hours
**Approx. Elevation:** 6,500 ft.
**Drop-offs:** Minor
**Sun Exposure:** Full sun
**Trail Type:** Rock/sand
**Restrooms:** None
**Water Source:** Stream/Seepage

This is a beautiful hike through Gambel oak, ponderosa pines, mountain rose, junipers, pinyon, and maples. It is absolutely beautiful during the fall months. Also along this path you will encounter two waterfalls and an old sawmill. To begin this hike you must exit the east entrance and travel 4.2 miles to a bend on the North Fork road (located 2.5 miles along Route 9 from the park entrance). From here start down the drainage and scramble along the rocks until you find an old trail on the right. Follow the trail for about .3 miles to the confluence and the old sawmill site, where you will find some woodpiles and old pieces of iron, all that remains of the sawmill. At the confluence you will find a waterfall dropping over ledges into some pools. Continue the hike downstream. You can bypass the pools on either side of the drainage and then drop back down into the bottom where you will follow the drainage down. The canyon soon becomes steeper and narrower, but is a beautiful walk. The water flow will increase as you continue downstream. Suddenly you will come to a 25-foot waterfall with a nice pool at the bottom. Bypass the falls by going right, around the big trees and back into the bottom via a small gulch. There is now a short, but very nice narrows and then you are out of the canyon.

*Horned lizard*

You will be able to see the East Rim Trail on a bench to your right; scramble up to the trail and follow it back to the east entrance. Remember, this trail is one way and will require the use of two vehicles for shuttling back and forth.

## Gifford Wash

**Difficulty:** Moderate
**Length:** 3 miles round-trip
**Average Time:** Two hours
**Approx. Elevation:** 5,500 ft.
**Drop-offs:** Minor
**Sun Exposure:** Full sun/shaded
**Trail Type:** Rock/sand
**Water Source:** None
**Restrooms:** Trailhead

This hike is a beautiful walk into a narrow canyon with a very diverse grouping of plant life, animal life, and rock formations. To begin the hike, park at the

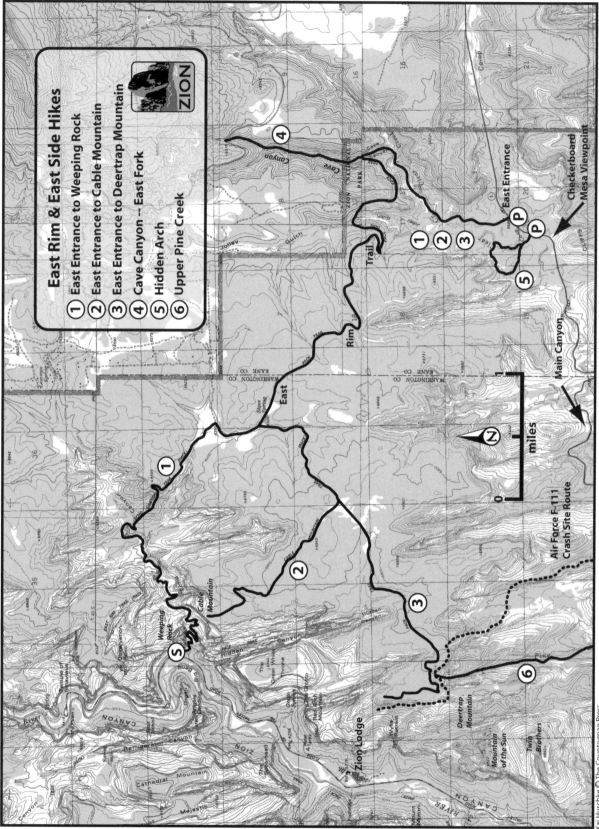

East Rim & East Side Hikes

1. East Entrance to Weeping Rock
2. East Entrance to Cable Mountain
3. East Entrance to Deertrap Mountain
4. Cave Canyon — East Fork
5. Hidden Arch
6. Upper Pine Creek

Kai Huschke © The Countryman Press

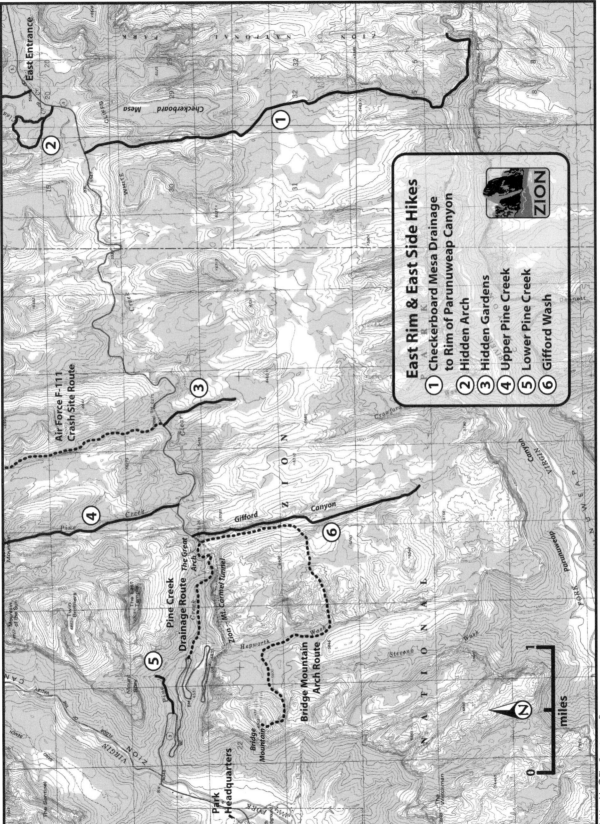

East Rim & East Side Hikes

1. Checkerboard Mesa Drainage to Rim of Parunuweap Canyon
2. Hidden Arch
3. Hidden Gardens
4. Upper Pine Creek
5. Lower Pine Creek
6. Gifford Wash

Kai Huschke © The Countryman Press

Canyon Overlook parking area just east of the East Tunnel entrance. Hike down into the Pine Creek drainage near the restroom and begin walking upstream. You will soon come to a dryfall where you will need to climb to the left, locating a path of use that will swing right at a level point with the top of the dryfall and then into Gifford Canyon. Continue upstream through a narrow canyon with sandstone cliffs. After a short distance you will find a rock dam, usually with some stagnant water at the base. The path will continue upstream for another .8 mile to the end of the canyon. To make the return trip, just retrace your steps. This canyon offers great solitude and is a great place to enjoy a picnic lunch. This canyon can be hazardous during inclement weather and is subject to flash flooding; check on current weather conditions before attempting this hike.

## Hidden Arch

**Difficulty:** Moderate
**Length:** 2 miles round-trip
**Average Time:** 1.5 hours
**Approx. Elevation:** 6,500 ft.
**Drop-offs:** Minor
**Sun Exposure:** Full sun
**Trail Type:** Rock/sand
**Water Source:** None
**Restrooms:** None

Hidden Arch was discovered and documented by the author in 1998. It is a beautiful "jug handle" arch located on the White Cliffs. The hike begins at the Checkerboard Mesa viewpoint parking area, where you will access the path at the northeast end of the rock wall. From here you will need to step up onto the wall and locate the path of use to the drainage below. Turn left and follow the drainage down to a confluence of a second drainage, turn right, and walk upstream. Follow the drainage for approximately .75 mile to where the drainage turns east you will then go left and climb the sandstone to the base of the White Cliffs, locating a path of use. Follow the path along the base of the cliffs, over rolling hills, until you have reached the tallest ridge leading to the left-hand side of the White Cliffs. Climb the ridge to the sandstone slope. From here you will have the best view of the arch. To locate the arch, look at the White Cliffs as a clock, the arch will be at about one o'clock and two-

thirds of the way up the face. It extends down from the second white buttress from the right. The arch looks like an elephant's trunk or a jug handle and is approximately 100 feet in length. It is very hard to find, hence the name "Hidden Arch." To make the return trip follow the ridgeline down about 100 feet and locate a path of use on the left side leading you back down to the drainage. Follow the drainage back to the parking area.

## Hidden Gardens

**Difficulty:** Moderate
**Length:** 1 mile round-trip
**Average Time:** One hour
**Approx. Elevation:** 5,500 ft.
**Drop-offs:** Minor
**Sun Exposure:** Full sun/shaded
**Trail Type:** Sand
**Water Source:** Seepage
**Restrooms:** None

One of the most beautiful of the hanging gardens can be found on this short hike into a very narrow slot canyon. The garden is lush with maidenhair fern, columbine, and other plant life. To begin the hike, park in the wide spot just at the west entrance to the short tunnel, drop into the Clear Creek drainage on the south side of the road, and begin walking upstream. The drainage can be muddy after a rainstorm and may have small pools that will need to be negotiated. Follow the drainage upstream about 30 meters; on your right will be a pine tree that is hiding the opening to a small fracture drainage. Enter the small canyon, which will require some bushwhacking. Follow the canyon upstream. The gardens will be present in several areas of this small canyon and the cliff formations are beautiful. The canyon is short and will require you to turn around and retrace your steps back to your car. Further exploration of the Pine Creek drainage in either direction is worth doing and can extend this hike by several miles if you would like to take a little longer to explore this beautiful drainage. This area is subject to flash flooding and should be avoided during inclement weather.

## Lower Pine Creek

**Difficulty:** Moderate
**Length:** 1.5 miles round-trip

**Average Time:** Two hours
**Approx. Elevation:** 4,100 ft.
**Drop-offs:** Minor
**Sun Exposure:** Full sun/shaded
**Trail Type:** Rock/sand
**Water Source:** Stream
**Restrooms:** None

This hike will offer you a look at the Pine Creek drainage. This area is full of wildflowers, ponderosa pine, hanging gardens, animal life, and beautiful waterfalls. On either side of you will be majestic cliffs, including Bridge Mountain of the right and the East Temple on the left. This is a great place to get in the water and cool off. This hike begins at the first switchback on the Zion–Mt. Carmel Highway going east from the Canyon Junction. The parking area is just before Pine Creek Bridge. As you begin the hike, take a close look at the colorful sandstone bridge of Pine Creek. The stonemason who constructed this bridge made an attempt to use every color of sandstone found

*Rock squirrel*

in Zion. The design is beautiful and provides a beautiful frame for a photo of Pine Creek. Continue the hike by walking upstream, staying as close to the river as possible. The path of use will be discovered as you walk along the stream and will cross the water several times. You can avoid getting your feet wet by choosing your route carefully. As you walk upstream, you will encounter several small waterfalls and pools, and finally end your hike at a waterfall of about 10 feet that falls into a beautiful pool worth a refreshing dip. To continue upstream from there may require technical gear and is not recommended. Retrace your steps for the return trip. This area is subject to flash flooding and can be hazardous during inclement weather. Be sure of weather conditions before entering the canyon.

## Upper Pine Creek

**Difficulty:** Moderate
**Length:** 2 miles round-trip
**Average Time:** Two hours
**Approx. Elevation:** 5,500 ft.
**Drop-offs:** Minor
**Sun Exposure:** Full sun/shaded
**Trail Type:** Sand/rock
**Water Source:** None
**Restrooms:** None

This hike is for the adventurous hiker looking to climb a fun boulder jam at the end of the canyon. The canyon is beautiful with diverse plant life, animal life, and cliff formations. The hike begins in Pine Creek drainage, east of the Canyon Overlook trail. Park in the last large pullout on the right going east after the Canyon Overlook "additional parking area." From here travel east following the road for about 200 yards, and drop into the drainage going north. Follow the creek bed upstream through the narrow canyon for about 1 mile until you reach the boulders that block the canyon; here you can climb the rocks and gain a vantage point of the canyon that offers great views of the drainage and Deertrap Mountain. At the top of the boulders the foliage is dense and farther exploration is limited. This is a short hike but a lot of fun if you like to climb rocks. This area is subject to flash flooding and can be hazardous during inclement weather, so be sure of weather conditions before entering the canyon.

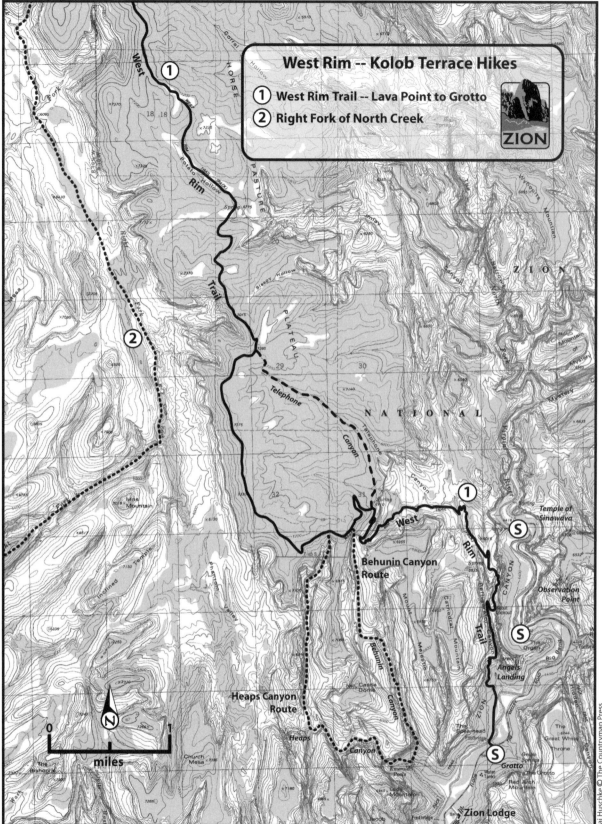

# West Rim—Kolob Terrace Hikes

## West Rim Trail—Lava Point to Grotto

**Difficulty:** Moderate
**Length:** 14.5 miles one way
**Average Time:** Nine hours
**Approx. Elevation:** 8,000 ft.–4,000 ft.
**Drop-offs:** Long at rim
**Sun Exposure:** Full sun/shade
**Trail Type:** Sand/rocks/paved
**Water Source:** Sawmill Springs/Cabin Springs
**Restrooms:** Lava Point

The West Rim Trail was constructed in 1925 (for details see the Angels Landing trail description, page 34). This trail is long and usually done in two days. To reach the trailhead, take the Kolob Terrace Road from Virgin City and travel 19.7 miles to Lava Point. From there follow the signs to the West Rim Trailhead. If the roads are muddy it is best to park at the Lava Point Campground and near site #3 you will find "Barney's Trail." This is a short connector trail that will take you to the West Rim Trail. The trail is along rolling hills until you descend into Potato Hollow. From there you will have some ascents up to Telephone Canyon Junction. The trail is then level until you reach Horse Pasture Plateau. From that point on you will have a continual descent to the Grotto. The trail takes you through many scenic vistas and views of Wildcat Canyon, Imlay Canyon, right and left forks of North Creek, Phantom Valley, and the Guardian Angels, Greatheart Mesa, and Mount Majestic. Ponderosa pine and other diverse vegetation play host to abundant wildlife. This area is the most popular backcountry destination and has campsites available.

The campsites are assigned by the Backcountry Office and will require a permit. This area may be impassable during winter months due to snow and muddy conditions.

## Wildcat Canyon from Lava Point

**Difficulty:** Moderate
**Length:** 6 miles one way
**Average Time:** Four hours
**Approx. Elevation:** 7,500 feet
**Drop-offs:** Minor
**Sun Exposure:** Full sun/shade
**Trail Type:** Rock/sand
**Water Source:** Route Spring
**Restrooms:** Lava Point

The Wildcat Canyon trailhead is located along the West Rim Trail, 0.2 miles from the trailhead. The trail will descend 450 feet from the West Rim Trail to the Wildcat Canyon Trailhead. There is also a 500-foot descent into and the same back out of Wildcat Canyon. This trail will take you through ponderosa pines, quaking aspen, Gambel oak, and grassy meadows. You will experience views of Russell Gulch, Pocket Mesa, Wildcat Canyon, and Lava Flows. The higher elevation boasts wildflowers later in the season and wildlife is abundant. Camping is permitted in this area; check with the Backcountry Office for information and permits. This area may be impassable during winter months due to snow and muddy conditions.

## Northgate Peaks from Kolob Terrace Road

**Difficulty:** Moderate
**Length:** 4 miles round-trip
**Average Time:** Two hours
**Approx. Elevation:** 7,500 feet
**Drop-offs:** Minor
**Sun Exposure:** Full sun/shaded
**Trail Type:** Rocks/sand
**Water Source:** None
**Restrooms:** None

The Northgate Peaks Trail is accessed from the Wildcat Canyon Trail. Start this hike from the Kolob Terrace Road/Wildcat Canyon Trailhead, which is located 15.3 miles from Virgin City. The trail will take you through forested areas to an overlook of the Northgate Peaks. Views of the North Guardian Angel and the Canyons of the Left Fork of North Creek are also found along this trail. Wildflowers are found later in the season and wildlife is abundant. This is a great day hike during the hot summer months because of the higher elevation. This area may be impassable during the winter months due to snow or muddy conditions.

## The Connector Trail

**Difficulty:** Moderate
**Length:** 4 miles one way
**Average Time:** Two hours
**Approx. Elevation:** 7,000 feet
**Drop-offs:** Minor
**Sun Exposure:** Full sun
**Trail Type:** Rocks/sand
**Water Source:** None
**Restrooms:** None

This hike is located 12.5 miles from Virgin City and connects the Hop Valley Trail to the Wildcat Canyon Trail, offering you the opportunity to complete a 38-mile hike from Lee Pass in the Kolob Canyons to the Grotto. This trail may be impassable during the winter months due to snow and muddy conditions.

## Left Fork of North Creek (Subway)

**Difficulty:** Strenuous

The Subway gets its name from the narrow canyon that resembles a subway tunnel, complete with two fault lines resembling train tracks, and the sound of water rushing through the canyon that sounds like a subway train. There are two ways to hike the Subway, from the bottom up or from the top down. This area is limited and allows only a certain number of visitors per day. This area also requires a permit even if done only as a day hike. Check with the Backcountry Office for details and permits.

### From the Bottom Up

**Length:** 8.8 miles round-trip
**Average Time:** Six hours
**Approx. Elevation:** 5,000 ft.
**Drop-offs:** Long
**Sun Exposure:** Full sun/shaded
**Trail Type:** Rock/sand
**Water Source:** Stream/seepage
**Restrooms:** None

The trailhead for Left Fork is located 7.9 miles from Virgin. The parking area is on the right-hand side of the road in the junipers. From the parking area you will travel through the junipers to the rim overlooking North Creek. From that point you will descend the cliff face via a crude trail to North Creek. Once you have reached North Creek, look for a landmark that will assist you in finding the trail back out of the canyon on your return trip. Follow the trail upstream. This trail will take you across the stream several times and you will get your feet wet. From that point you will be about 3 miles from the Subway formation. The trail offers wonderful rock formations, wildflowers, and wildlife. The North Fork Drainage is strewn with boulders but offers beautiful water features as you make your hike. Located approximately 1.4 miles from the bottom of your descent are some dinosaur tracks on the left-hand side of the creek. As you reach the Subway you will be delighted by the narrow canyon formations and water flows. You will not be able to proceed beyond the Subway because of large boulder jams in the drainage. This area is subject to flash flooding. Check with the Visitor Center for current weather conditions before attempting this hike. This area may also be impassable during winter months due to high water, snow, and muddy conditions.

### From the Top Down

(See the description in the chapter on canyoneering, page 63.)

## The Right Fork of North Creek

**Difficulty:** Strenuous

There are two ways to hike the Right Fork of North Creek—from the bottom up to "Double and Barrier Falls" or from the top down through the "Great West Canyon." The Right Fork of North Creek is one of the most beautiful and least explored areas of the park. Along this route there are numerous pools, waterfalls, and cascading water features. The route also offers diverse plant and animal life. This route is difficult and should only be attempted by experienced hikers. The routes in and out are hard to find and require basic route, finding knowledge. Both routes are subject to flash flooding and can be very dangerous. Check with the Backcountry Office for weather information and required permits before attempting either route.

### Bottom Route to Barrier Falls

**Length:** 7 miles one way
**Average Time:** Five hours
**Elevation:** 6,000 ft.
**Sun Exposure:** Full sun/shaded

**Drop-offs:** Long
**Trail Type:** Rock/sand
**Water Source:** Right Fork
**Restrooms:** None

The trailhead is located 6.9 miles from Virgin City via the Kolob Terrace Road. A small dirt parking area is located on the right side of the road, tucked into the juniper trees. From the parking area, hike .2 miles southeast to the rim of the canyon and look for a rock cairn marking the spot to begin your descent to North Creek. The trail is steep and works its way down through the lava slope. Once you have reached North Creek, follow it north to the confluence of the right and left forks. Walk up the Right Fork along the south side of the stream. Up 1.3 miles from the confluence you will find Trail Canyon to the south, farther upstream you will find some old corrals. Continue upstream, where you will find a side canyon from the north. Continue following the stream for about .8 miles to where the canyon narrows at a pool. From there continue to follow the streambed for about 1 mile to Double Falls, a beautiful set of waterfalls cascading into an emerald pool. Continue on the south side of the pool through a brushy trail around the falls. Watch for poison ivy in this area. The route becomes more difficult from this point to Barrier Falls because of large boulders that will require some scrambling. Barrier Falls is .5 mile farther upstream; several beautiful waterfalls will be passed along the way. Barrier Falls is named appropriately because you are blocked from any farther travel upstream. This area is subject to flash flooding; check current weather conditions before entering this canyon. Check with the Backcountry Office for camping permits and other requirements before making this hike.

### Top Route via Great West Canyon

(See the description in the section on canyoneering, page 63.)

## South Guardian Angel

**Difficulty:** Strenuous
**Length:** 7 miles round-trip
**Average Time:** 12 hours
**Approx. Elevation:** 6,500 ft.
**Drop-offs:** Long
**Sun Exposure:** Full sun

**Trail Type:** Rock
**Water Source:** North Creek
**Restrooms:** None

This trail is a beautiful hike through the sandstone cliffs of the North Creek Drainage. Views of the Left Fork, Greatheart Mesa, Russell Gulch, and the Guardian Angels make the trip worth all the sweat and effort. The area is covered with ponderosa pine, pinyon, junipers, and abundant wildflowers. This area is also cougar (or mountain lion) country, and is home to other wildlife. The hike is long, hard, and hot. The area is rugged terrain with many obstacles to negotiate such as sandstone cliffs, steep slopes, and little cover from the hot sun. Hikers wanting to attempt this route should be in good physical condition and have good route-finding skills, and a basic understanding of canyoneering requirements.

To begin this hike, travel from Virgin 15.3 miles to the Wildcat Canyon trailhead, follow the trail approximately 1 mile to the head of Russell Gulch, the first drainage going east after the Northgate Peaks Junction. Drop into the drainage and begin working your way downstream. To the north is a large unnamed mesa with a large narrow canyon draining to the west. When you reach this confluence, climb east out of the Russell Gulch and continue walking southeast below the Mesa. Direct your route toward Greatheart Mesa. Continue walking until you find a sandstone drainage near the southeast end of the unnamed mesa that will allow you to descend to the Left Fork of North Creek, allowing you to make the stream crossing (you will need to find a suitable crossing route). Once you have made the crossing, follow the stream course downstream until you have reached a drainage entering from the south. From here climb the sandstone drainage and follow it until it levels out. Now ascend the steep ridge to the west until you have reached the base of a steep sandstone cliff. Follow the base of the cliff north until you have walked the northwest end of it and then begin walking southeast toward the top of the rise. Here you will be able to see the South Guardian Angel. From here walk south and west across the sandstone; many obstacles will make this walk very difficult. Stay to the high side of the cliffs and continue working your way to a sandstone drainage that drains Greatheart Mesa. Once at the

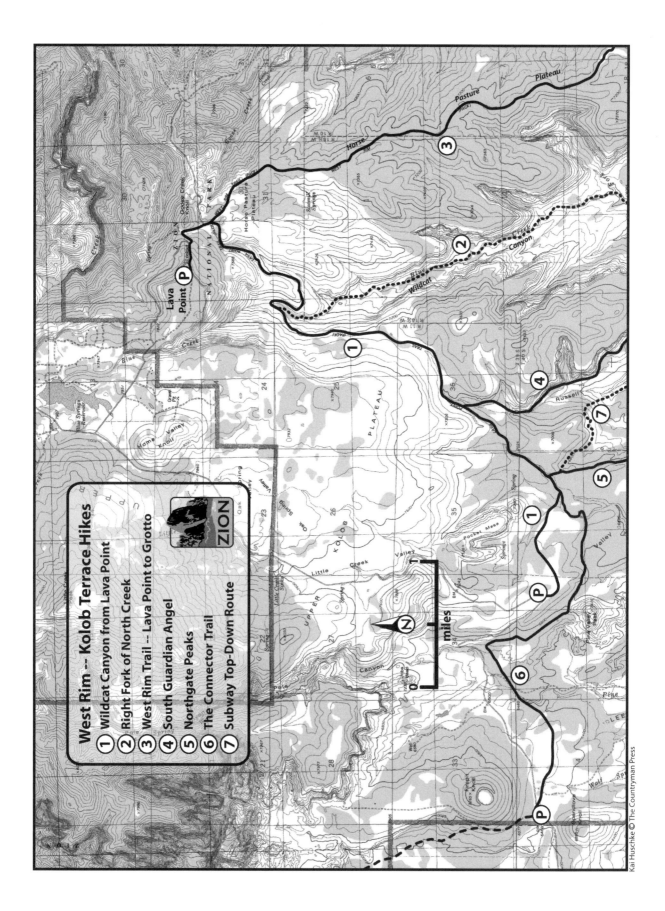

West Rim -- Kolob Terrace Hikes

1. Wildcat Canyon from Lava Point
2. Right Fork of North Creek
3. West Rim Trail -- Lava Point to Grotto
4. South Guardian Angel
5. Northgate Peaks
6. The Connector Trail
7. Subway Top-Down Route

ZION

N

miles

Kai Huschke © The Countryman Press

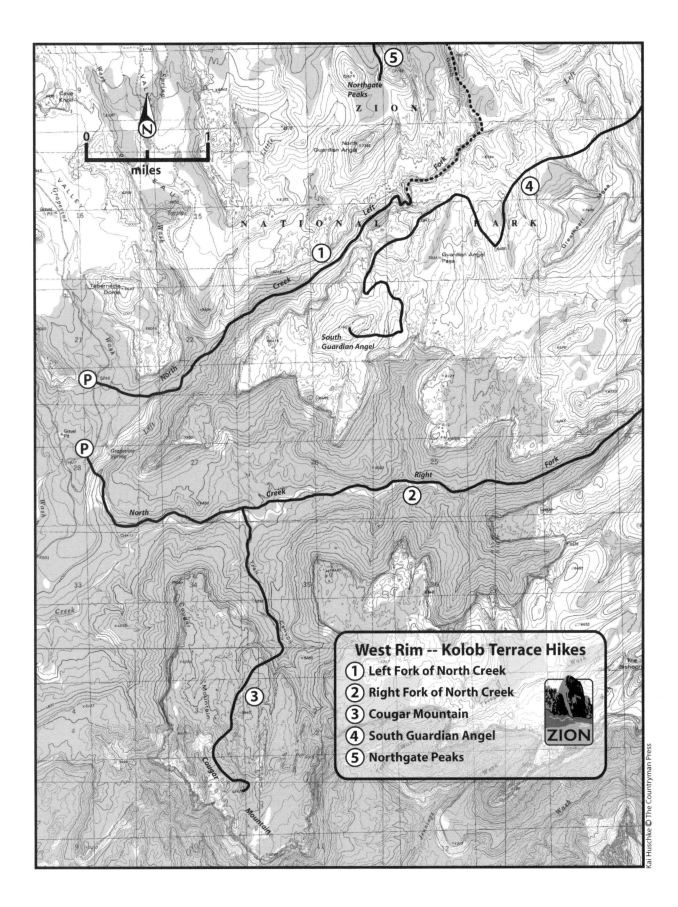

West Rim -- Kolob Terrace Hikes

1 Left Fork of North Creek
2 Right Fork of North Creek
3 Cougar Mountain
4 South Guardian Angel
5 Northgate Peaks

ZION

Kai Huschke © The Countryman Press

drainage, work your way downstream to the confluence of Left Fork. Once you have reached the confluence, work your way downstream to the drainage (on your left). Descending from the South Guardian Angel, follow the drainage upstream until you have reached the base of South Guardian Angel and then begin to work your way north along the base until you reach an area where you can look down into a drainage flowing toward the Right Fork of North Creek. Start your steep climb up the sandstone in a westerly direction. The final climb to the top will be on the northeast slope to the base of the eastern peak. From here go south until you find the final, 60-foot steep sandstone slope that will allow you to reach the top. The views from this magnificent vista will make the long, difficult, hot, and time-consuming hike worth the effort. Return by retracing your steps. This area is rugged and can be dangerous during inclement weather. Check with the Backcountry Office for current weather conditions, required permits, or other information before attempting to do this hike.

## Cougar Mountain

**Difficulty:** Strenuous
**Length:** 5 miles round-trip
**Average Time:** Six hours
**Approx. Elevation:** 6,400 ft.
**Drop-offs:** Long
**Sun Exposure:** Full sun
**Trail Type:** Rock/sand
**Water Source:** Right Fork
**Restrooms:** None

This is a beautiful hike to the mountain named for the wildcats in the area. The canyon is rugged and has a diverse community of plant life, animal life, and cliff formations. From the top of Cougar Mountain you will have views of the Bishopric, South Guardian Angel, Tabernacle Dome, and surrounding drainages. The trailhead is located 6.9 miles from Virgin via the Kolob Terrace Road. A small dirt parking area is located on the right side of the road, tucked into the juniper trees. From the parking area, hike .2 miles southeast to the rim of the canyon and look for a rock cairn marking the spot to begin your descent to North Creek. The trail is steep and works its way down through the lava slope. Once you have reached North

Creek, follow it north to the confluence of the right and left forks. Walk up the Right Fork along the south side of the stream; 1.3 miles from the confluence you will find Trail Canyon to the south. From here follow the drainage upstream, staying in the drainage. There are numerous obstacles that can be easily bypassed by alternate routes. Approximately 1 mile upstream you will reach a fork in the stream. Follow the left fork, where you will need to do some bouldering until you reach a 40-foot dryfall. Traverse to the right until you are level with the top of the dryfall and then reenter the drainage. Continue upstream; the drainage is fairly wide at this point. Begin to climb left out of the drainage after about .25 mile when you can see some animal trails leading you out of the bottom. Follow the animal pathways until you have reached the saddle below Cougar Mountain. Travel east toward the base, traversing the ledges until you are about 30 feet below the rim. Locate a chute with several small caves left of the saddle rim. Here you will be able to continue to the top using the chute as a pathway. For the return trip, retrace your footsteps. This area is rugged and may be impassable during inclement weather. Check with the Backcountry Office for current weather conditions, permits, or other requirements before attempting this hike.

## Kolob Canyons

One of the least visited and most beautiful areas of Zion National Park are the Kolob Canyons. The massive cliffs of red sandstone leave you breathless. This area is highly recommended and should be explored to its fullest. Kolob Canyons is accessed via I-15, exit 40. To reach Kolob Canyons from Zion Canyon Visitor Center drive west on Route 9 to La Verkin, take Highway 17 north to I-15 and travel north again to exit 40. Driving time is about one hour. Backcountry permits and other information can be obtained from the Kolob Visitor Center just off the exit.

### Timber Creek Overlook Trail

**Difficulty:** Moderate
**Length:** 1 mile round-trip
**Average Time:** .5 hour
**Approx. Elevation:** 6,300 ft.
**Drop-offs:** Minor

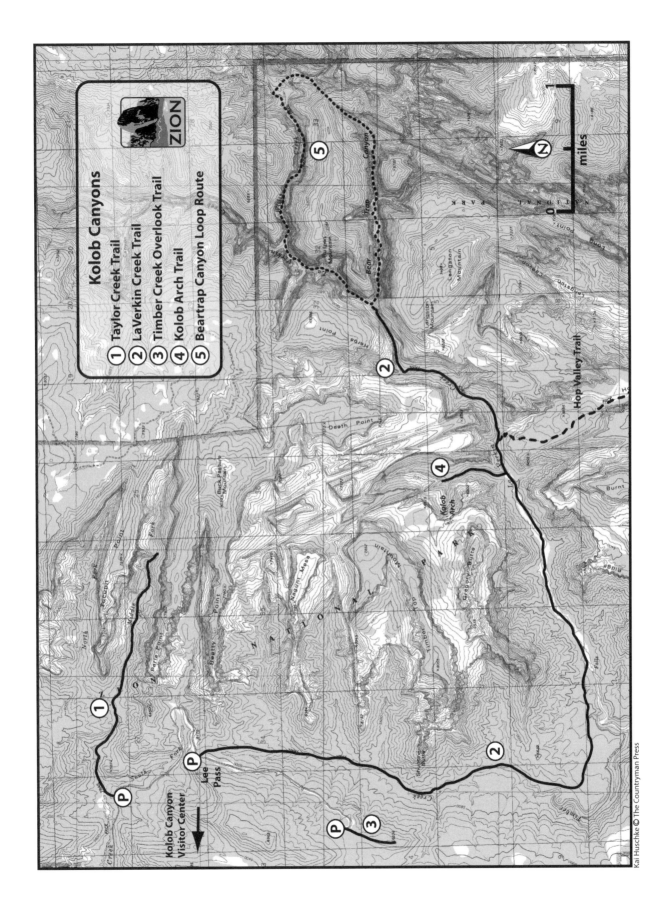

**Sun Exposure:** Full sun
**Trail Type:** Rock/sand
**Water Source:** None
**Restrooms:** Trailhead

This trail is accessed from the end of the 5-mile scenic drive. The trail will take you along the ridge to a small peak that will give you a great view of the La Verkin Creek Valley, Timber Creek, Kolob Terrace, and the Pine Valley Mountains. The trail is rocky and travels through the pinyon and juniper trees. Wildflowers are present during late spring and early summer because of the higher elevation. The pinyon and Steller's Jays are common birds in this area; other wildlife may also be observed. The fall colors are beautiful from this vantage point. This area may be impassable during the winter months due to snow and muddy conditions.

## Taylor Creek Trail

**Difficulty:** Moderate
**Length:** 5 miles round-trip
**Average Time:** Four hours
**Approx. Elevation:** 5,500 ft.
**Drop-offs:** Minor
**Sun Exposure:** Some sun/shaded
**Trail Type:** Rock/sand
**Water Source:** Stream
**Restrooms:** Trailhead

This is a very nice walk along the Middle Fork of Taylor Creek, a small stream that works its way through the pinyons and junipers. There is a diverse community of plant and animal life along this trail, with the towering cliffs of Tucupit and Paria Points above you. The trail is rich with natural history and will be rewarding from start to finish. Along the trail you will encounter two pioneer cabins; the first belonged to the Larsen family and the second is an old fire cabin. The trail becomes a little more rough as you progress down the trail due to the terrain. Continue to travel upstream, watching for the trail; try to stay on the main pathway. After you have reached the old fire cabin, the trail will bend to the right, where you find Double Alcove Arch, a large natural grotto with spectacular colors and rich hanging gardens of golden columbine. The area is cool and a very nice place to take a break before heading back. This area may be impassable during the winter months due to snow and muddy conditions. Camping is not allowed.

## Kolob Arch Trail

**Difficulty:** Strenuous

There are two ways to hike to Kolob Arch, from Lee Pass along the Kolob Canyons scenic drive or from Hop Valley along the Kolob Terrace Road. Either hike will offer a great opportunity to observe beautiful sandstone formations, plants, and wildlife. At the end of either trail you will see Kolob Arch, possibly the largest freestanding arch in the world, measuring 310 feet.

### From Lee Pass

**Length:** 7.2 miles one way
**Average Time:** Four hours
**Decent:** 699 ft.
**Drop-offs:** Minor
**Sun Exposure:** Full sun/shaded
**Trail Type:** Sand/rocks
**Water Source:** Springs along route
**Restrooms:** Trailhead

The La Verkin Creek Trail is accessed from Lee Pass, located 3.5 miles up the Kolob scenic drive from the Visitor Center. From Lee Pass to La Verkin Creek you will lose elevation as you work your way into the valley floor. The trail will traverse through the Timber Creek valley with massive sandstone cliffs above you. The trail will intersect with La Verkin Creek at the old corral and becomes fairly level from that point to Kolob Arch Junction. The trail is very sandy and makes for difficult walking. The trail will have many diverse plant life communities along the way, pinyon/juniper as you begin, sagebrush, and finally cottonwoods along the stream. Look for the hanging gardens along seepages. At Kolob Arch Junction you will be .6 miles from the arch viewpoint. The trail parallels a tiny stream, winding through boulders and onto a tree-covered bench where you will see the arch by looking up. Other destinations of that area are within a short walk and worth the effort. From the junction it is a short walk to Hop Valley junction. Continue to walk upstream (about 2 miles) to Beartrap Canyon; a narrow spring-fed stream will take you to a waterfall about .3 miles upstream. Technical gear is required to go beyond the falls. Hiking Kolob Arch is best done in two days, camping is available in designated campsites.

Camping is this area requires a permit and may be obtained at either the Kolob Canyons Visitor Center or the Zion Canyon Backcountry Office. This area may be impassable during winter months due to snow or muddy conditions.

### From Hop Valley Trailhead

**Length:** 6.7 miles one way
**Average Time:** Four hours
**Descent:** 1,000 ft.
**Drop-offs:** Minor
**Sun Exposure:** Full sun
**Trail Type:** Sand/rock
**Water Source:** Stream/spring
**Restrooms:** Trailhead

To access the Hop Valley Trailhead, drive 12.5 miles from Virgin up the Kolob Terrace Road. The trail begins north of the parking area and will travel through sagebrush, cactus, and Gambel oak. Firepit Knoll is to the west and Red Butte to the northwest. The trail is sandy for about 1.5 miles, at which point you will reach the hikers' gate. This is an entrance to private land; please respect the owner's property. From there the trail will follow an old four-wheel-drive road with cedar posts leading the way to a steep descent into Hop Valley, where the roadway disappears. Walk downstream to Langston Canyon, which enters from the east. Shortly past that point you will see a cattle fence with a hikers' gate on the bench to the east of the stream. Continue in the wash until you find a sign pointing to the trail climbing the hill on the west side of the canyon. From the top of the hill you will begin a long series of switchbacks into the La Verkin Creek Valley. Once you have reached La Verkin Creek, walk downstream a short distance to Kolob Arch Junction. From there it is .6 miles to the arch viewpoint. From the Hop Valley Trail Junction you can walk upstream into Beartrap Canyon (about 2 miles), where a beautiful waterfall can be seen. Travel beyond the waterfall requires technical gear. This hike is best done as a two-day excursion. Camping is permitted in designated campsites only (see Lee Pass description), and can be obtained from either of the Visitor Centers.

## Southwest Desert Trails

In the Southwest corner of Zion National Park resides one of the most interesting and diverse environments of this area. The elevation is the lowest found within park boundaries, at 3,640 feet. It hosts desert terrain that is well worth exploring. Desert plants and animals inhabit this area and have adapted to water-conserving lifestyles. The area is best avoided during the summer months due to full sun exposure and high temperatures. The following descriptions are the most popular routes in this area; however, many trail combinations are possible to enhance your hiking experience.

## Chinle Trail to Coalpits Wash

**Difficulty:** Moderate
**Length:** 8.1 miles one way
**Average Time:** Four hours
**Elevation:** 4,000 feet
**Drop-offs:** None
**Sun Exposure:** Full sun
**Trail Type:** Sand/rock
**Water Source:** Coalpits Wash
**Restrooms:** None

To access the Chinle trailhead travel on Highway 9, approximately 3.5 miles from the south entrance. In between Springdale and Rockville you will find "Anasazi Plateau," a housing development on the right-hand side of the road. Parking for the trail is located a short distance up the development roadway on your right. From that point you will walk through private property until reaching the park boundary. The trail leads you through the desert with many beautiful colors of sand and rock formations. About 3 miles from the trailhead you will walk through the Petrified Forest. Look for large log formations buried in the trail and some beautiful pieces of petrified logs scattered throughout the area. You will soon find a sign marking the old Scoggins Stock Trail. Early pioneers used this trail to move cattle. The trail will terminate at Coalpits Wash, a usually reliable water source. If you would like to farther explore this area you can continue upstream of the wash and spend another full day hiking into the cliff areas of Zion. At Coalpits Wash walk downstream toward water cascading over the Shinarump formation. Continue

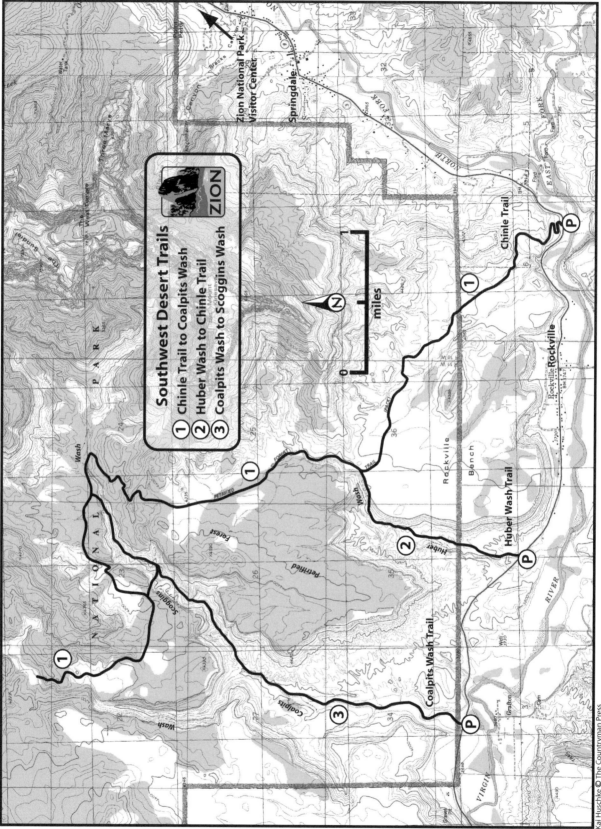

Kai Huschke © The Countryman Press

*West Temple from Chinle Trail*

downstream about 100 yards and you will discover a beautiful alcove with hanging gardens and a small spring. Return routes can be made via the Coalpits Wash or Huber Wash (see trail descriptions for information). Camping is allowed in this area, though a permit is required from the Backcountry Office. This area is very muddy during wet weather.

## Huber Wash to Chinle Trail

**Difficulty:** Moderate
**Length:** 2.5 miles one way
**Average Time:** Two hours
**Elevation:** 4,000 ft.
**Drop-offs:** Minor
**Sun Exposure:** Full sun
**Trail Type:** Sand/rock
**Water Source:** None
**Restrooms:** None

To access Huber Wash, travel south on Highway 9 approximately 1 mile south of Rockville. You will see the Huber Wash sign on the right-hand side of the road. Parking is on the north side of the wash. After parking, go through the gate and walk north along the wash. Please leave all gates closed as you pass through them. Once you have reached the park boundary, drop into the wash and follow it from there on. The rock formations are beautiful in this area and plant and animal life are abundant. Continue walking north until you are stopped by a dryfall. Look up on the wall to your right and you will find a logjam of petrified wood. You can climb the slope to get a good look at the jam. Please leave it alone so others may enjoy it. To access the Chinle trail, you will need to backtrack about 100 yards where you can work your way up the boulders to the mesa. From the top of the mesa, head northeast until you connect with the Chinle Trail.

Camping is permitted in this area; for information and permits, see the Backcountry Office. This area is very muddy during wet weather.

## Coalpits Wash to Scoggins Wash

**Difficulty:** Moderate
**Length:** 1.8 miles one way
**Average Time:** Two hours
**Elevation:** 4,000 ft.
**Drop-offs:** Minor
**Sun Exposure:** Full sun
**Trail Type:** Sand/rocks
**Water Source:** Coalpits Wash
**Restrooms:** None

To access Coalpits Wash, drive south on Highway 9 approximately 2.7 miles south of Rockville. You will see the Coalpits Wash sign on the right-hand side of the road. Park on the north side of the wash, then, after parking, go through the hikers' gate and follow the wash to the confluence of Scoggins Wash. This hike will offer a desert environment and great views of the canyons to the north. Plant and animal life will be found along the trail. Several routes may be taken to access different locations in this region. A favorite route from the confluence is to the Coalpits Alcove, located an additional 1.6 miles up Coalpits Wash. This route can be difficult because of the boulders in the wash bottom. You can avoid most of the difficulty if you stay left of the wash. Within this area a small stream passes through the large boulders, creating waterfalls, pools, and cascades. This portion of the hike will take a considerable amount of time. Plan on a full-day hike to complete this and the return trip. This area can be dangerous during heavy rains and may be muddy.

*A day in the Narrows*

# 7. Backcountry Canyoneering Route Descriptions

## Virgin River Drainage

### Orderville Canyon

**Difficulty:** Strenuous, Technical
**Length:** 12.5 miles
**Average Time:** 10 hours
**Sun Exposure:** Full sun/shaded
**Water Source:** Stream
**Equipment Needed:**

- One 50-ft. 8mm rope
- Harness
- Prussiks or ascenders
- 50 ft. of webbing
- Bolt kit
- Dry bags
- Survival equipment

*Rappelling the cliffs*

Typically the best months for hiking this canyon are June, July, and September. However hiking can be done anytime with proper planning and equipment. The fall months are beautiful with color. This hike is usually done as a long day hike as camping sites are limited along the hike route.

This is a narrow slot canyon, which flows into the Virgin River (lower portion of the Narrows), and is a very difficult hike. This hike should be reserved for the experienced hiker, as it requires good physical strength and endurance. The route has many obstacles along the way such as logjams, deep pools, waterfalls, and slippery mud. To begin this hike, exit the park at the east entrance and travel 2.5 miles on Highway 9 to the North Fork Road. Turn left and drive north 11.9 miles to a dirt road that turns right. To the east of the road you drove in on is a series of dirt roads. You will want to take the road that is lined on both sides with Gambel oak. Follow this road a short distance to a wire corral. Four-wheel-drive vehicles can proceed from this point to the bottom of the hill and then turn left on another four-wheel-drive road and follow it to the bottom of Orderville Gulch, where you will cross a stream. Continue on the road along the stream until you cross the stream again. Park about 100 yards from this point. Follow the path (roadway) through the rabbit brush to where a prominent canyon enters from the left. Continue until you

can drop off the bench into the drainage. Follow the drainage about .5 mile to the beginning of Orderville Canyon. At this point you will find a 125-foot dry fall. You can bypass this dry fall by going back upstream and walk south to locate a place that will allow you to descend the slope. At the base of the slope will be a bench that you can follow, which leads to a descent into the streambed near a drainage entering from the left. From this point on, the hike will remain in the streambed. As you make this hike you will pass many side canyons. Just stay in the streambed heading downstream. You will arrive at a set of narrows that is the boundary of Zion National Park; in this area you will have your first major obstacle. A boulder about 15 feet tall is in the streambed and will have to be navigated. You can best do this by climbing down the right side if the area is dry; it is best to anchor a line and use it to climb down. As you continue downstream you will encounter more water in the streambed from side tributaries. You will soon enter some incredible narrows. As you exit the narrows you will find the second major obstacle, two large boulders; you can bypass them by going to the left or right side,

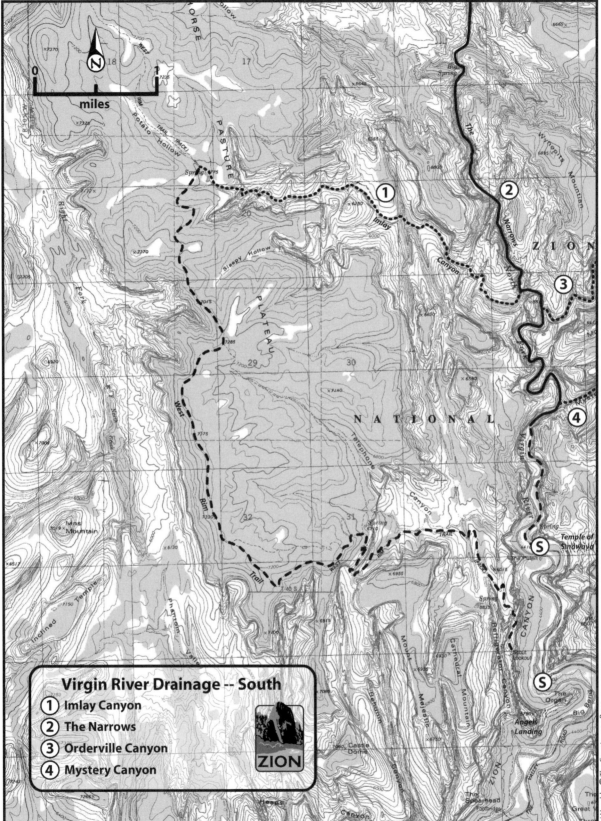

Virgin River Drainage -- South

1. Imlay Canyon
2. The Narrows
3. Orderville Canyon
4. Mystery Canyon

ZION

Kai Huschke © The Countryman Press

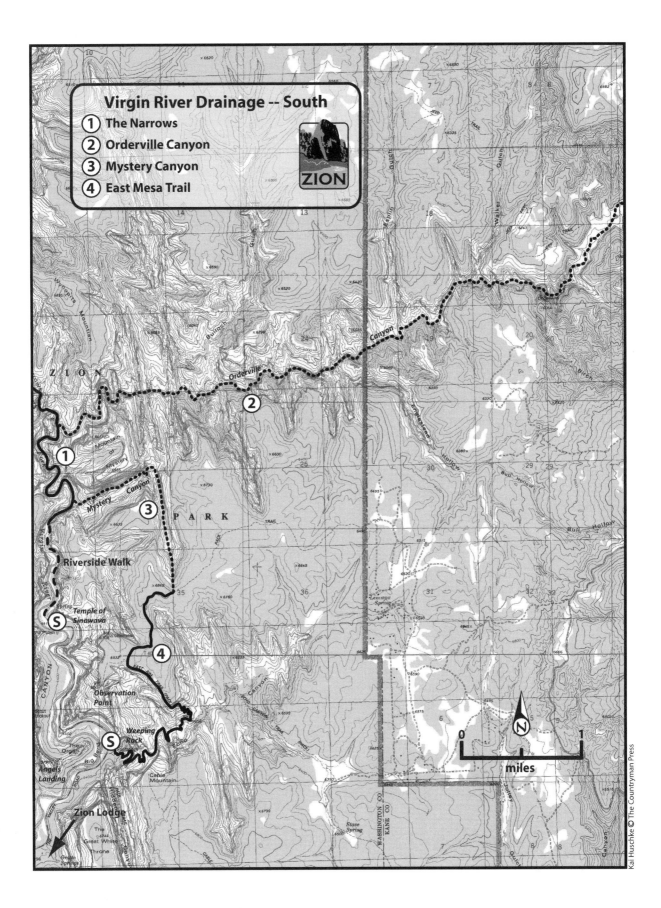

Virgin River Drainage -- South
1 The Narrows
2 Orderville Canyon
3 Mystery Canyon
4 East Mesa Trail

ZION

depending on which is a better route at the time. You will need to drop about 15 feet; use your rope for assistance. Beyond this point there will be several more obstacles that will need to be navigated the canyon will then open up with many seeps and springs. From this point it is just a short walk to the confluence of the Virgin River Narrows. This area is subject to flash flooding and may be hazardous during inclement weather. Check with the Backcountry Office for required permits, current weather conditions, and other requirements before attempting this route.

## Imlay Canyon

(Imlay Canyon Only)

**Length:** 3 miles one way
**Average Time:** 15–20 hours
**Sun Exposure:** Full sun/shaded
**Water Source:** Stream
**Equipment Needed:**
- Two 165 ft. 8mm ropes
- Two 40 ft. 8mm ropes
- Harness
- Prussiks or ascenders
- 50 ft. of webbing
- Bolt kit
- Wet suit
- Dry bags
- Survival equipment

This hike is very difficult. Hikers electing to do this route should be strong swimmers in good physical conditionand have route-finding, canyoneering, rappelling, and rope-management skills. The route is beautiful and will challenge even the most seasoned mountaineer. Beginning from Potato Hollow, follow the trail around the left side of the pond to the rim of Imlay Canyon. Stay on the north side of the canyon and make your first rappel from a large ponderosa about .2 miles from the head of the canyon. The first rappel will be about 160 feet down a low-angle slope to another large pine. Another 120-foot rappel will get you to the canyon bottom. From here you will make a 150-foot rappel through four waterfalls and a plunge pool where you will begin the walk downstream through a short narrows. Stay left when you exit and work your way back into the canyon bottom. Make a short rappel, stay left of the bottom, and work your way to an exposed rollover. Make the 40-foot

rappel to a large pine tree on the left side of the steep pour over; use the tree to make a 110-foot rappel down to a small lip. On the lip you will find anchors for your next rappel of 140 feet down a slick wall. You will then be in the bushy canyon bottom and will need to bushwhack downstream with some downclimbing and short rappels until you come to an area with high ground and a good campsite for the night. Continue downstream, negotiating and swimming several pools to the next rappel—a 50-foot drop into an alcove where the canyon will bend to the right. From here you will experience many rappels, swims, and pools before reaching the final rappel into the Virgin River. The canyon will offer many challenges and will take some time to do. Choose your route carefully and at rappel locations look for anchors. Some have them; some do not. As you approach the confluence with the Virgin River you will be making a series of rappels equal in scenery to no other place in the park. The canyon will bend left and a final rappel and swim will get you to a solid rock platform at the end of the canyon. From the platform make your final rappel into the Virgin River Narrows—look for a bolt on the left side of the platform. The rappel is about 125 feet, and mostly free hang. The Temple of Sinewava is about a two-hour walk downstream. This area is subject to flash flooding and can be hazardous during inclement weather. Check with the Backcountry Office for current weather conditions, permits, and other requirements before attempting this route.

## Mystery Canyon

(Loop from Weeping Rock to Virgin Narrows)

**Length:** 7 miles
**Average Time:** 6–10 hours
**Sun Exposure:** Full sun/shaded
**Water Source:** Stream
**Equipment Needed:**
- Two 165 ft. 8mm ropes
- Harness
- Prussiks or ascenders
- 50 ft. of webbing
- Bolt kit
- Dry bags
- Survival equipment

This route offers some fantastic canyon views, wildflowers, and water features. Those choosing to do this hike should be in good physical condition and have route-finding, canyoneering, rappelling, and rope-management skills. Begin hiking from the Weeping Rock trailhead and follow the trail toward Observation Point. At the junction of East Rim and East Mesa trails, follow the East Mesa Trail for about .75 mile to the head of Mystery Canyon. Be sure of your route by using a topographic map; it is easy to drop into the wrong canyon. From the head of the canyon follow the path of use to the rim of the canyon and onto the descent trail. Make your way down the path, being very careful through the steep descent and loose rock. Once in the bottom locate the boulder in the creek bed with an anchor attached. Use the anchor to make a 15-foot rappel; begin walking downstream. The canyon will narrow quickly with a 60-foot rappel; locate the anchor on the left-hand side. From here you will have to negotiate five more rappels, about 30 feet or less, all having bolted anchors. From here there are two more rappels that can be bypassed by staying right above the seventh rappel and climbing over the slope to a gully and then back into the drainage. The canyon will now begin to open up and walking is easy down to a landslide where there will be a pond or bog. Climb the landslide and continue downstream to the next 30-foot rappel. Two bolts can be found on the flat shelf to the right of the stream. Continue downstream, where the canyon will narrow; you will have to negotiate some pools before reaching the next rappel, a 110-foot drop from a ledge on the left side of the canyon and into a pool requiring a float off. Look for the bolts after traversing the ledge about 40 feet. From the pool continue downstream to a 10-foot drop into a pool that will require swimming about 15 feet. After the swim, it is just a short distance to the end of the canyon and your final 120-foot rappel. Located on a tree to the left of the waterfall is a set of slings. Make the rappel to the Virgin River. From here it is a short walk back to the Temple of Sinawava.

## Kolob Creek
(Kolob Creek Canyon only)

**Length:** 15 miles one way
**Average Time:** 15–20 hours
**Sun Exposure:** Full sun/shaded
**Water Source:** Stream/river

**Equipment Needed:**
- Two 165 ft. 8mm ropes
- Harness
- Prussiks or ascenders
- 50 ft. of webbing
- Bolt kit
- Wet or dry suit
- Dry bags
- Survival equipment

This hike is very difficult. Hikers electing to do this hike should be in good physical condition, be strong swimmers, and have route-finding, canyoneering, rappelling, and rope-management skills. The route has major obstacles throughout it such as Class III Slopes, Class IV Chimney, steep waterfalls, and cold pools. NOTE! NOTE! NOTE! This hike is only feasible during low/no water conditions. Early summer months are usually the best time to attempt this hike. Do not attempt to make this hike without checking with the Washington County Water Conservancy District (435-673-3617) to verify water-release conditions for Kolob Creek. It is your responsibility to contact the district office. Check with the Backcountry Office for current weather information, needed permits, and other requirements before making this hike. A permit will not be issued if the water flow is higher than 5 cubic feet per second due to dangerous undertows and water currents.

To access this hike, take the Kolob Terrace road from Virgin to the Blue Springs Reservoir. About .5 mile past the reservoir you will find Kolob Creek flowing under the road; park in the wide spot on the right near there. As you begin your descent from here, you should be able to see the waterfall flowing off the basalt cliffs. Follow the basalt cliffs down to the drainage by staying left of the falls. As you make your way to the drainage and continue downstream, you will be doing some bushwhacking for a couple of hours until you reach the first 6-foot rappel into the creek. This rappel can be made from a small pine tree on the left. Once in the bottom you will be wet for several miles as you make your way downstream through the water. Just below the first rappel will give you a feel for the water challenges that lie ahead; a pool and short slot will be a 15-foot swim. The canyon tightens from here and begins its deep descent. The second rappel will be short and off a tree. The third rappel will be from the logjam to a pool below. The fourth rappel will be downstream a short distance. Look for the anchor from a sling around a boulder in the middle of the stream. From here continue working your way downstream to the next rappel of three pools. A single rope can be used to negotiate the three pools, about 60 feet. Continue downstream to a narrow twisting canyon where you will make a free rappel down a narrow slot into the pool below. From here there is a succession of four quick rappels through pools requiring you to swim. Continue downstream to where the canyon opens a little. This will be an exposed double-rope rappel; look for the bolts over the drop-off. From here down there is a succession of about 10 short rappels and then the canyon opens up to a brushy, tree-covered area.

*Moonrise along Kolob Terrace Road*

Continue downstream of Kolob Creek, negotiating boulders and the stream until you reach a waterfall dropping about 8 feet into a pool; you will have to swim to get through it. Shortly after this pool you will find the canyon narrows to sheer walls on both sides. Work your way downstream, negotiating through the water. There will be several pools that will require walking or swimming through. You will eventually reach the largest pool of this hike. It has a 20-foot waterfall and drops into a deep pool. On the boulder near the falls you will find a bolt you can use to rappel into the pool. Continue downstream from there where you will need to farther negotiate boulders, dry falls, and pools through some beautiful narrows until you reach the confluence of the Virgin River. Near the confluence are campsites 5 through 12 (see the Narrows description for campsite size and location). You will welcome the campsites and opportunity to rest after making this grueling hike. This hike is very dangerous, subject to flash flooding, and time-consuming. Check with the Backcountry Office for weather conditions and other requirements before attempting to do this hike.

# East Rim Routes
## Air Force F-111 Crash Site
(Short Tunnel to Deertrap Mountain)

> **Length:** 3 miles one way
> **Average Time:** 10 hours
> **Sun Exposure:** Full sun
> **Water Source:** None reliable
> **Equipment Needed:**
> - 1 50 ft. 8mm rope
> - Harness
> - Bolt kit
> - Survival equipment

On July 11, 1973 at 3 PM an Air Force F-111 jet crashed above the Zion Lodge below the rim of Deertrap Mountain. The pilots were able to eject to safety in a capsule and landed west of Lady Mountain. Even today, some of the aircraft still remains. This is a fun but strenuous day-hike and requires route-finding, canyoneering, and rope-management skills. To begin the hike, park at the pullout on the west side of the short tunnel. Drop into the drainage on the north side of the road and begin following the drainage upstream. The route is tough walking with many obstacles that will need to be negotiated as you slowly climb toward the top. The steepest part of the hike, at the end of the drainage, will require some hit-and-miss route finding as you scramble and climb to the top. Once on top, travel straight north until you reach the Deertrap Mountain Trail. Follow the trail west to Deertrap, where you will see the trail going over the top of the sandstone cap. Bypass the cap by staying to the east side and walk below the cap to the Grotto Drainage. Continue on around the east side of drainage until you can look down into the drainage and see a ledge about 20 feet down. A rope-assisted climb down to the ledge can be done from several cracks near here. Once on the ledge, follow it north to the crash site. The site is hard to see and you will have to be right upon it before realizing you have reached it. Several burnt tree stumps still remain to assist in marking your route. Retrace your footsteps for the return trip. This area is dangerous and should not be attempted during inclement weather. Check with the Backcountry Office for current weather conditions, permits, or other required information before attempting this hike.

## East Side Routes

### Bridge Mountain Arch

(Canyon Overlook Parking to Bridge Arch)

**Length:** 5 miles one way
**Average Time:** Six hours
**Sun Exposure:** Full sun
**Water Source:** None
**Equipment Needed:**
- One 165 ft. 8mm rope
- Harness
- 25 ft. of webbing
- Bolt kit
- Survival equipment

This hike offers spectacular views of the Pine Creek Canyon and the Temples of the Virgin. You will be required to make your own trail through the rock ledges, junipers, pinyon and ponderosa pines. Desert bighorn sheep are found in this area, so keep watch for them.

This hike is very difficult and should only be attempted by persons who are in good physical condition and who possess route-finding, climbing, and rope-management skills.

To begin the hike, park at the Canyon Overlook parking area just east of the East Tunnel entrance. Hike down into Pine Creek Drainage near the restroom and begin walking upstream. You will soon come to a dry fall where you will need to climb to the left, locating a path of use that will swing right at a level point with the top of the dry fall and then into Gifford Canyon. Follow the canyon floor about 1 mile and then begin climbing the sandstone on the right side. Work your way through the ledges as you stay under the prominent dome on the skyline. This area can be very difficult in finding a route up—the route you choose may dead-end and you will need to try somewhere else. Continue to work your way up until you reach a large natural bowl. Continue hiking west as you stay right of the drainage until you reach the head of the bowl. Climb to the plateau to the south through the broken ledges. Once on the plateau, head north to a west-flowing canyon and begin to descend into the bowl by whatever route you can find. At the base of the bowl, climb approximately 200 feet up the north side to a fin with some hoodoos on it. Continue climbing to the saddle between the hoodoos; this may require technical gear. Once you have reached the saddle, you will again hike to the bottom of the canyon. Once in the bottom, continue down the canyon until you reach Hepworth Wash. Follow the wash downstream (north) past the canyon that drains to the west. Just beyond this canyon there is a canyon that drains east of Bridge Mountain. From here begin walking northwest to the first natural corridor to the north of Bridge Mountain. Climb the corridor and through the notch and then down the other side to a loose rock bench covered in oak. From the bench walk left to a 30-foot chimney where you will need to be experienced in climbing. The use of technical gear is required. Continue the hike up the fracture (about 100 yards) and then go right to where you will climb down into a hanging valley and walk south to the aspen trees. From the aspens it is only 200 yards south to the arch. To make the return trip, retrace your route. This area is dangerous and subject to falling rocks, lightning, and other hazards. Check with the Backcountry Office for weather conditions, required permits, and other regulations before attempting this hike.

## Pine Creek Drainage

(Pine Creek Canyon Only)

**Length:** Approx. 1.2 miles
**Average Time:** Four hours
**Sun Exposure:** Full sun/shaded
**Water Source:** Stream/seepage
**Equipment Needed:**

- Two 150-ft. ropes
- Harness
- 50 ft. of webbing
- Bolt kit
- Dry bags
- Survival equipment

Nicknamed "Fat-Man's Peril," this hike is a spectacular narrows hike right from the beginning. Anyone attempting this hike should be good physical condition possess rappelling and rope-management skills, and strong swimming ability. The route is accessed from the Canyon Overlook parking. Drop into the drainage near the restroom and follow it downstream, underneath the bridge, and into the narrows. The narrow section can change greatly with every storm so be prepared to negotiate logjams, mud, pools, etc. Continue into the narrows until you reach the first rappel, about 20 feet. Continue to the second rappel, also about 20 feet; both areas have decent anchors. Farther downstream you will find the third rappel, which will require dropping into a deep pool. You will need to swim if recent rain has fallen. Once through the pool, continue downstream. The area is often very muddy. The next rappel will be about 80 feet and the last will be about 100 feet onto a ledge. From this point down the canyon opens up. Stay left and negotiate the small cliffs and ledges. Once you have passed this point, work your way back to the drainage and continue to

*Sagebrush lizard*

follow it downstream until you find a route leading out of the drainage to the second switchback on the Zion–Mt. Carmel Highway. This area is subject to flash flooding, falling rocks, and other hazards. Check with the Backcountry Office for weather conditions, permits, and other requirements before attempting this route.

# West Rim—Kolob Terrace Routes

## Behunin Canyon

(Loop from Grotto to Emerald Pools)

**Length:** Approx. 7 miles
**Average Time:** 10 hours
**Sun Exposure:** Full sun/shaded
**Water Source:** Stream potholes
**Equipment Needed:**

- 330 ft. of parachute cord
- Two 165 ft. 8mm ropes
- 120 ft. of webbing
- Bolt kit
- Medium angles
- Baby angles
- Figure eights and another belay device
- Dry bag
- Survival equipment

To begin, this hike follows the West Rim trail to the final switchback leading up to West Rim Springs. From West Rim Springs, begin walking down the wash. There will be a lot of bushwhacking and some minor obstacles for about 1 mile. At the point where the canyon begins to turn east you will encounter several pools and a large drop-off. Stay to the left and as low to the drainage as you can until you reach a ponderosa pine. From here make a rappel back down into the drainage. Continue downstream to the first long rappel; look for a large ponderosa with a webbing anchor on it. The rappel is about 120 feet. Continue downstream to a second large ponderosa with a webbing anchor and make a 150 feet rappel to a level bowl in the middle of the face. From here make the next rappel of about 120 feet to the bottom. Once in the bottom the walking is fairly easy down to the next rappel of about 85 feet. Look for the anchor on your right. Continue downstream; again the walking is easy for a short distance and then you will encounter several pools and minor obstacles. Most of the pools can be bypassed by traversing above them. You may need to use a handline in some areas to get back to the drainage bottom, but none are too difficult. When you have reached the next rappel, you will need to climb to the left and find a small tree with a webbing anchor. Make the rappel of about 40 feet to the first pool. With careful routing you can avoid getting wet. Once around the pools you will be able to see the end of the canyon about 100 yards away. The final rappel to the Emerald Pools trail will consist of a three-stage rappel; the first will be about 50 feet to a ledge, and then a second rappel of about 90 feet to a larger ledge. From here you will make your final rappel to the bottom. Look for the bolt below a chockstone about 6 feet below the ledge; the rappel is about 160 feet with the last 130 feet consisting of freehanging. Once at the base, you will boulder scramble to the Emerald Pools Trail. This area is subject to flash flooding and can be hazardous during bad weather. Before attempting this route, check with the Backcountry Office for current weather, permits, and other requirements.

## Heaps Canyon

(Loop from Grotto to Emerald Pools)

**Length:** Approx. 8 miles
**Average Time:** 15–20 hours
**Sun Exposure:** Full sun/shaded
**Water Source:** Stream
**Equipment Needed:**
- 330 ft. of parachute cord
- Two 165 ft. 8mm ropes
- 120 ft. of webbing
- Bolt kit
- Medium angles
- Baby angles
- Figure eights and another belay device
- Dry bags
- Full wet suit
- Survival equipment

To begin the descent into Heaps Canyon, leave West Rim Springs and take the West Rim Trail to the head of Heaps Canyon. Enter the canyon on the east side where you will need to scramble down a slope to a 100-foot rappel into the bottom of the canyon. The anchor point is a large fir tree. Follow the canyon down to a chimney system. This will require about five rappels using fixed anchors, chock stones, or pinches. At the bottom of the chimney it is fairly easy walking to another drop, although if you stay right

you can walk around it. Stay on the right side of the canyon, traversing the slick rock to a large fir tree. From there, a 100-foot rappel will drop you back into the main canyon. Continue downstream to a 60-foot rappel. From that point you will encounter several drop-offs and deep pools. You can climb right to a ridge and bypass the deeper pools. You can see the crossroads from the ridge. Look for a slick rock descent to a large fir tree. From here, make the 100-foot rappel back into the canyon. Continue downstream, where you will be negotiating waist-deep pools all the way to the crossroads. The crossroads have good campsites above the waterline and are recommended as your first-night-camp location. From the crossroads, continue downstream to where the canyon narrows. Staying left, climb up the canyon and walk about .25 mile to a tree with slings. Make the rappel back into the canyon and you will be less than .25 mile from the narrows. When you enter the narrows be prepared to swim. This area has pools that require swimming distances of nearly 300 feet. You will find several short rappels on logjams with drilled pins and webbing. Continue downstream to where the canyon opens up. Stay left and you will soon come to a 65-foot rappel that will take you to the end of the canyon. Hike left over a 35-foot boulder, then to the right to a chimney and down to a tree. Make a 40-foot rappel off this tree to another tree, where you will make a 150-foot rappel to a stance with four bolts. From here you will make your final rappel of 320 feet to the bottom. This area is subject to flash flooding and can be hazardous. The water is cold and the obstacles are difficult. Route descriptions may change after every storm. Check with the Backcountry Office for weather conditions, permits, or any other requirements before attempting this hike.

## Lady Mountain

(Ascent/Descent from East Edge)

**Length:** 7 miles round-trip
**Average Time:** Eight hours
**Sun Exposure:** Full sun
**Water Source:** None
**Equipment Needed:**
- 50-ft. rope
- Chocks
- Plenty of water
- Survival equipment

Lady Mountain, so named because the likeness of a woman can be found on the north face, has a long history in the park and makes for a spectacular route. The Lady Mountain Trail was constructed by the Park Service in 1925 and consisted of 1,400 chiseled rock steps, two ladders, and 2,000 feet of cable. The trail was very popular with visitors. However, due to difficulty in maintaining the trail and many visitor injuries, the trail was disbanded in 1978. The following route description mimics that historic trail. The route is difficult and should only be attempted by experienced hikers.

The route begins from the Middle Emerald Pools Trail. From the trailhead follow the path approximately .5 mile to where a sign will read DANGER: ROLL NO ROCKS—PEOPLE BELOW. Hike west up the steep slope. A faint trail remains and is seldom used. From the base of the sandstone cliff look for the footholds carved into the rock and climb to the top of the inclined bench, about 35 feet. From there continue climbing to the top of the cliffs, approximately 300 feet, where you will find some switchbacks. Climb to the top left switchback. Here you will be at the base of the next cliff. Look for some handholds and use them to friction the cliff to a crevice, about 250 feet. Climb the crevice about 26 feet, and then traverse the rim to the south until you reach the rock staircase. Climb the staircase about 120 feet, and again traverse south about 1,000 feet, where you will begin to ascend to the base of the cliff. From the cliff base, use a belay to ascend about 35 feet. Follow the cliff top to a crevice where you will ascend about 120 feet; go left and climb up, going around the gully on the south. Continue this route until you have passed through a narrow cleft in the rock. The route will now go north along a ridge. Follow the ridge to a saddle where you can see the summit of Lady Mountain. Follow the narrow ridge about 250 feet to the base of a cliff on the southwest side of Lady Mountain, and continue this route until you have reached the top of the mountain. At the top, look for a brass orientation marker that identifies the prominent points visible from this lookout point. Retrace your steps to return. This area can be hazardous in wet weather and during thunderstorms. It is inaccessible during the winter months. Check with the Backcountry Office before attempting this hike for any hazards, needed permits, weather conditions, or other information that may be useful.

# Left Fork of North Creek (Subway)

### From the Top Down
- **Length:** 9.5 miles one way
- **Average Time:** Eight hours
- **Sun Exposure:** Full sun/shaded
- **Water Source:** Stream/seepage
- **Equipment Needed:**
- One 50-ft. 8mm rope
- Harness
- 50 ft. of webbing
- Bolt kit
- Dry bags
- Survival equipment

This route is much more difficult than from the bottom up. Only hikers with canyoneering, rappelling, and route-finding experience should attempt this hike. The starting point for this hike is the Wildcat Canyon Trailhead located 15.3 miles from Virgin. You will need to make transportation arrangements because you will end at a different location than where you start. Follow the trail to the North Gate Peaks Trail Junction and follow the North Gate Peaks Trail about 0.1 mile to the top of the hill. Locate the trail to the left and follow it to the rim of Russell Gulch. You will now descend about 200 feet along the ledges to the south side of the drainage. Stay to the right of the drainage and descend the sandstone slopes to the drainage and cross the streambed. Walk east approximately 0.2 mile to where you can see the bottom of Russell Gulch. Work your way down the sandstone slope about 200 feet to the crossing of Russell Gulch. Head south to a pink-colored sandstone saddle with a pair of hoodoos. Once on the saddle, hike southeast down a sandstone bowl parallel to Russell Gulch crossing two drainages. As you cross the second drainage, look for a ridge to the south and follow game trails to the top. Follow the ridge to a steep 200-foot descent into Cleft Chute Route to a plunge pool near the confluence of Russell Gulch and Left Fork. Walk down North Fork through a boulder field to a second plunge pool. You will need to navigate a 12-foot drop. On the right there is a crack between the boulder and canyon wall. Belay if needed and descend to the plunge pool. Continue downstream to a right-hand turn where you will need to swim through a 30-foot pool and then a 15-foot pool. From this point you will round a bend and find a spring that marks the beginning of Left Fork Creek. Just beyond this point you will find a narrow gorge that will require negotiating the stream. On the left-hand side, climb 10 feet to a ledge system where you will need to squat and crawl along the ledge to a sandstone slope. Work your way back down to the drainage. A ponderosa pine will give you a belay point to assist you down. Downstream from this point you will find Keyhole Falls, a 10-foot drop. Loop your rope through the runner bolted to the right side and then lower yourself into the pool below. Continue downstream to a waterfall and pass it on the right along a ledge system. Farther downstream the creek will flow into a crack and cascade 15 feet into the Subway. Stay to the left following a ledge system, double your rope through the runners bolted in the sandstone, and lower yourself to the stream below. From this point forward you will no longer need your rope to negotiate the trail. Continue downstream about 2 miles where you will find the confluence of Little Creek. An abandoned trail in the lava flow can be seen from this point. Do not take this trail out of the canyon. Continue downstream until you find a second lava flow on the right side of the canyon. Look for the trail to work its way up the canyon to the Left Fork Trailhead. This area is subject to flash flooding and may be impassable during the winter months due to snow, cold water, and muddy conditions.

## Right Fork of North Creek

### Top Route via Great West Canyon

**Length:** 17.5 miles one way
**Average Time:** 14 hours
**Sun Exposure:** Full sun/shade
**Water Source:** North Creek
**Equipment Needed:**
• One 120-ft. 8mm rope
• Harness
• Prussiks or ascenders
• 50 ft. of webbing
• Bolt kit
• Dry bags
• Survival equipment

The Great West Canyon Route is one of the most difficult hikes in the park. Experienced hikers will find it challenging and rewarding. Only hikers with canyoneering, route-finding, rope-management, and rappelling skills should attempt this route. To access the trailhead, drive 19.7 miles to the Lava Point Campground and access the West Rim Trail. Follow the trail to the Wildcat Canyon trail. Follow Wildcat Canyon Trail to the bottom of the plateau, where you will find Blue Creek. From this point leave the trail and follow the drainage down Wildcat Canyon. The path will require climbing over logs, bushwhacking, and boulder hopping. Continue to follow the drainage, passing the first side canyon found on your left. Proceed to the second side canyon entering from the left where you will climb to a ridge on the right side of the drainage. Follow the sandy ridge to a third canyon that enters from the left, then drop into the drainage and climb the low saddle on the left side of the streambed. From the saddle, continue downstream to the Left Fork of North Creek. Look for a large twin hoodoo on the hillside; continue hiking to the left of the drainage through the meadows and stands of Gambel oak. The oak is thick and is better to bypass them however possible. Make your way to the crest of the hill where you will find a small peak. Stay left of the peak and work your way through the Gambel oak to the east side of the peak and then drop into the small drainage. Continue along the small drainage until you connect with the Right Fork drainage. From this point you will want to follow the drainage until you can find an area to the right where you can climb out and onto the slopes. Work your way up the slopes to the crest of the ridge. Follow the ridge southeast for about .5 mile, where you will see the canyon open up and walking can be done with less bushwhacking. You will come to the giant staircase and will want to continue your walk in the drainage until you reach a narrow fracture and the drainage has a steep drop. You will need to belay at this point to assist you down the fracture. Stay left and descend the slopes to a ridge that leads to a sandy wooded area; descend again into the drainage. Walk the drainage until you enter a fissure where you will want to stay right and leave the fissure before dropping through the crack. Work your way down into the drainage and continue downstream to Right Fork

*Climbing the falls in Orderville Canyon*

numerous obstacles. Stay left of the big ones and you should be able to avoid any rope-assisted descents. You will eventually reach the Grand Alcove, easily identified by the large overhang forming a natural amphitheater. You can follow the streambed, but you will get wet and it is very difficult, or you can go to the cliff side of the overhang and rappel to the shelf below using the existing bolts and then make a second rappel to the alcove floor using a tree as your anchor. From the floor continue downstream to the last major obstacle, Barrier Falls. Look for the bolt near the falls and rappel to the bottom. Continue downstream using the best route you can find until you reach Double Falls, stay left, and work your way around the falls and back to the drainage. From the bottom of the falls, continue downstream about 5.6 miles to the confluence of the Right and Left Forks. Continue downstream from there until you find the lava flow on the right; pick a route up through the lava to the canyon rim. You may be able to find previous pathways marked with cairns. Once on top of the rim it is a short walk to the roadway and you will be able to find the Right Fork parking area if you happen to miss it on your way out. This area is subject to flash flooding. Check with the Backcountry Office for current weather conditions, camping permits, and other requirements before attempting this hike.

## Kolob Canyon Routes

### Beartrap Canyon Loop

**Length:** Approx. 10 miles
**Average time:** Eight hours
**Sun Exposure:** Full sun/shade
**Water Source:** Stream/seeps
**Equipment Needed:**
- One 100-ft. 8mm rope
- Harness
- 50 ft. of webbing
- Bolt kit
- Survival equipment

This area is beautiful and makes a great day hike from a base camp along La Verkin Creek near the Kolob Arch Junction. Those wishing to make this trip should have route-finding, rappelling and rope-management skills. Begin the route from the confluence of the LaVerkin Creek and Beartrap. To reach the confluence from the Hop Valley Junction continue up-

Canyon. Continue downstream to a large boulder; climb under the boulder and onto the shelf. Stay to the right of the pool and continue to the next large boulder, where you will need to again climb underneath—this time on the left side. Continue downstream to a major obstacle—the "Black Pool." This pool may be as long as 100 yards and is very cold. The best route around the pool is to the left, where you will need to navigate some ledges to a point where you can rappel back into the drainage or shallow end of the pool if it's very large. Continue downstream to a waterfall. Stay left and climb along the edge until you see a fracture that will allow you to descend back into the drainage. Continuing downstream you will encounter

stream of the LaVerkin for about 2 miles; from there you continue to follow the stream another mile or so to the confluence of Willis Creek. From this point, follow Willis Creek upstream until the canyon opens to a wide valley, look for a drainage on the right, less than 400 yards after entering the valley. Follow the drainage (which drops down from the Hardscrabble) approximately .5 mile to a saddle on your right. Work your way up, through the Gambel oak to the lowest section of the saddle and then, staying left, walk the ridge to a point where you can drop into the Beartrap Drainage. You may have to use a rope to assist your descent if you can't locate an accessible route to scramble down. Once in the drainage, continue your descent into the bottom of Beartrap Canyon. You will be required to negotiate several large boulders using your rappelling gear. The descent is difficult and will be time consuming, but it's well worth the effort. From the bottom of Beartrap, continue downstream by the best route found. A side canyon on the left will be about .5 mile downstream and then approximately .5 mile beyond there you will need to rappel a waterfall. Stay to the left of the falls to make your descent. Continue downstream to your starting point. This area can be hazardous during wet weather and is subject to flash flooding. Before attempting this route, check with the Backcountry Office for current weather forecast, permits, and other requirements.

# 8. Climbing, Horseback Riding, and Biking

## Climbing

Zion Canyon offers some of the best climbing in the world. The scenery is beautiful and the routes challenging. The sandstone cliffs offer unique challenges to the experienced climber and are not recommended for amateurs. The climbs are on open cliff faces and typically over 2,000 feet in length.

### Route Descriptions

There are many different routes available within the park. You may obtain route descriptions at the Backcountry Office' they have been compiled by previous climbers and are not guaranteed to be accurate. The route books are organized into sections of the park and contain route maps and descriptions. You may want to research climbing routes through some of the published books available in stores. Once you have completed a climb in the park you are welcome to make changes to existing route descriptions or create a new one if completing a new route.

### Sport Climbing

Zion National Park does not have sport climbing. Sport climbers can find climbing locations in the nearby Snow Canyon State Park, located northwest of St. George. The Snow Canyon Ranger Station can provide location and route information. The second area for sport climbing is in the Virgin River Gorge on Interstate 15, south of St. George. The Virgin River area is newly developed and contains climbs from 5.9 to 5.14, with most of the climbs in the 12 to 13 range. Check with the Bureau of Land Management (BLM) Visitor Center in St. George for farther information.

### Short Climbs

Zion has many short climb routes in the park but currently does not have maps for all of them. One good area to look for a short climb is near the West Tunnel entrance. Check out the map on the wall opposite of the kiosk at the entrance. The Kolob section of the park also has some good short climbs. Check with the Visitor Center there for route locations.

*A big wall climb*

### Bouldering

Zion has two accessible bouldering areas in the main canyon. The first is a boulder with many excellent problems and an intense traverse, located about 40 meters west of the south entrance.

The second is Drilled Pocket Boulder, across the street from the campgrounds and a bicycle information sign. Look for a slab boulder with an obvious south-facing crack.

Other boulders are strewn throughout the park and offer some good problems. There is no real restriction on choosing a boulder. Be aware that sandstone is soft and the flakes may peel off when weight is applied. Be sure of the integrity of the boulder before climbing.

## Top Roping

Because of the 2,000-foot cliffs and lack of anchors, top roping is not recommended. If top roping is attempted, trees that are used should be carefully chosen as some trees have very shallow root systems or may be in weak crevices and can give way under your weight.

## Route Closures

Before attempting to make any climb within the park, check with the Backcountry Office for current route closures. Every year from February to August some routes are closed to protect nesting peregrine falcons. Several areas are routinely closed. They include the following: the Great White Throne, Cable Mountain, Court of the Patriarchs, and Tunnel West.

## Permits

Permits are not required for day climbs but are required for all overnight bivouacs. Permits may be obtained from the Backcountry Office the day of or the day prior to climbing.

## Parking and Access

When you have chosen a route, inform the Backcountry Office of your route location and where your vehicle will be parked. The shuttle system must be used whenever possible for routes located in the main canyon during the months the shuttle operates. One exception to this is if you plan to make a day hike round-trip requiring you to leave before the first shuttle and returning after the last. Talk with the Backcountry Office for needed special permits.

## Climbing Safe

Throughout the year the best conditions for climbing are between March and May, then again between September and November. Summer months are extremely hot and not recommended. Remember that sandstone is soft and very weak when wet; avoid hiking during inclement weather or in damp areas. Do not attempt to support your weight on thin wafer-like holds and brush the sand off rocks before making friction moves. Inspect all preexisting bolts or pins to ensure their integrity.

## Minimum Impact Climbing

When you have chosen a route, use established trails to gain access to the starting point. Camping is not

*Attempting a free-climb*

permitted at the base of the climb or in your car. If using chalk, add red pigment to lessen the visual impact. All human and other waste should be bagged and carried out. DO NOT drop your waste. You may not remove vegetation from cracks or remove fixed pins. While climbing remove all old, worn rope and equipment found along the route. It is illegal to use power drills for setting bolts. Do not climb routes where you are above trails that may have hikers on them.

# Horseback Rides and Stock Use

## Main Canyon Trail Rides

Guided horseback rides are conducted daily from the Emerald Pools trailhead along the Sand Bench Trail. Rides consist of one-hour and half-day trips. Contact Zion Lodge to schedule a ride.

## Private Stock Use

For years horses have been used to explore Zion's rugged country. Even today you are permitted to use private stock in many areas of the park. Those areas include the following: La Verkin Creek, Hop Valley, Wildcat Canyon, West Rim (above Cabin Springs), Cable Mountain, Deertrap Mountain, and the Sand Bench from November through February. Off-Trail areas include Coalpits Wash, Huber Wash, Scoggins Wash, and Crater Hill.

Stock animals currently permitted in the backcountry are horses, mules, and burros. Animals not permitted are llamas, dogs, camels, or any other pack animals. Group sizes are limited to a group of no more than six animals. Permits are not required for any day trips but are required for overnight outings. Permits may be obtained from the Backcountry Office the day of or the day prior to making the trip. Stock must be hobbled or tethered to minimize damage to vegetation. Stock must be fed with certified weed-free hay one day prior to entering the backcountry to reduce the spread of noxious weeds and exotic plants. In all areas where trails are present, stock must remain on the trails. Free trailing or loose herding is not permitted. Keep stock at least 100 feet from all water sources.

## Bicycling

Biking opportunities in Zion are limited to the Pa'rus Trail and main roadways. The use of bicycles on established trails, off-road, or in the backcountry is strictly prohibited. However, some of the best mountain biking in Utah can be found a short distance from Zion near the town of Rockville. Gooseberry Mesa, as well as other areas, offers some fantastic trails and beautiful scenery. Several biking companies in Springdale can provide you with more information, bike rentals, and maps.

*Emerald Pools waterfall*

# 9. Bryce Canyon, Grand Canyon North Rim, and Other Destinations Within 60 Miles

## Bryce Canyon

Head northeast from Zion via Highway 9 to Mt. Carmel Junction, then turn north on Highway 89 to Highway 12, then on to Bryce Canyon. The trip will take about two hours from Zion Canyon Visitor Center.

### Bryce Canyon History

Bryce Canyon consists of thousands of delicately carved pinnacles or spires, called "hoodoos," in the pink cliffs of this western edge of the Pausaguant Plateau. The colors of the natural amphitheater formations are brilliant. Bryce Canyon consists of more than 60 million years of geologic history. On a geologic time scale, Bryce is a relatively young formation and began in the late Cretaceous period. The formation, known as the Claron formation, has been deposited, uplifted, and eroded by millions of years of geologic processes. Water, wind, snowmelt, and other forces have eroded away millions of tons of sedimentary deposits and left behind the spires, pinnacles, and rock

*Natural bridge, Bryce Canyon National Park*

formations you see today. For centuries, Paiute Indians lived near Bryce Canyon, using the plateau for hunting and fishing. In the fall of 1875 Ebenezer Bryce became one of the first settlers of this area and operated a cattle ranch. Soon it became known as Bryce's Canyon. During this time, life was a matter of survival and little credence was given to this area for its beauty. Bryce was asked one time what he thought of the area and his response was, "It's a hell of a place to lose a cow." Bryce Canyon became a National Monument in 1923 and was established as a National Park in 1928.

### Visit Recommendation

A visit to Bryce Canyon should start at the Visitor Center and museum to learn more about the park and to obtain park information. If you only have one day, the following is recommended to get the most out of your visit:

**Sightseeing Only.** If you take the 18-mile scenic drive, I recommend traveling all the way to the end, Yovimpa Point, before making any stops and then start making your way back along the scenic drive. All pullouts are

---

### TRAVEL DISTANCES FROM ZION NATIONAL PARK

**National Parks**

**Arches:** 330 miles, six hours
**Bryce Canyon:** 82 miles, two hours
**Canyonlands:** 320 miles, six hours
**Capitol Reef:** 200 miles, four hours
**Grand Canyon North Rim:** 120 miles, three hours
**Lake Powell:** 95 miles, two hours

**Destination Cities**

**Cedar City, UT:** 58 miles, 1.5 hours
**Las Vegas, NV:** 157 miles, three hours
**Los Angeles, CA:** 427 miles, six hours
**Page, AZ:** 116 miles, two hours
**Phoenix, AZ:** 395 miles, six hours
**Salt Lake City, UT:** 310 miles, five hours
**St. George, UT:** 42 miles, one hour

*North Rim of the Grand Canyon*

then on the right-hand side for easy access. My recommendations for don't-miss viewpoints are:

- Yovimpa and Rainbow Point
- Natural Bridge View Point
- Bryce Point
- Sunset Point
- Fairyland Point

To visit each of these points will take a good portion of the day. Restrooms are available at several points and the picnic tables at Sunset Point are a good place for lunch.

**Hiking Trail Recommendations.** Hiking Bryce Canyon is a great way to see the canyon from deep inside the beautiful formations. Keep in mind that Bryce Canyon is nearly 8,000 feet in elevation and hiking can be strenuous. My recommendations for hiking trails are:

- Sunset to Sunrise (easy): .5 mile
- Sunset to Inspiration (easy): .7 miles
- Sunset to Sunrise via Navajo Loop/Queens Garden Trail (moderate): 2.9 miles
- Tower Bridge (strenuous): 3 miles
- Fairyland Loop (strenuous): 8 miles

There are other trails to hike and if you are spending several days in this area, talk with Park Rangers about other hikes, including backcountry hikes.

# Grand Canyon North Rim

Head northeast from Zion via Highway 9 to Mt. Carmel Junction, turn south on Highway 89 to Kanab, then continue south on Highway 89A to the North Rim. The trip will take about three hours from Zion Canyon Visitor Center. Note: The North Rim is only open from May to October. It is recommended that you call or check with Zion before leaving for the North Rim.

The North Rim of the Grand Canyon is my favorite way to visit the Canyon. Of the 5 million visitors to the Grand Canyon each year, only 10 percent travel to the North Rim. Representing billions of years of geologic history the Grand Canyon is one of nature's greatest wonders. The park elevation is above 8,000 feet, giving you a completely different environment than that of the South Rim.

## North Rim History

John Wesley Powell made the first recorded scientific exploration of the Grand Canyon. His trip down the uncharted Colorado River into the depths of the Grand Canyon must have been an adventure of a lifetime. The beauty of the canyon is much the same today as it was when Powell made his first journey through the Grand Canyon in 1869. It is known that the Desert Archaic people inhabited the area nearly 4,000 years ago. These people were nomadic hunters and gatherers. Following these people the Anasazi inhabited the area until about A.D. 1,200. The Paiutes followed about 100 years later. 1n 1776, Fathers Escalante and Dominguez mapped the region and wrote of its majesty. In 1919, an act of Congress established the Grand Canyon as a National Park.

## Visit Recommendation

Visiting the North Rim should start at the Visitor Center to learn more about the park and to obtain park information. If you only have one day, the following is recommended to get the most our of your visit:

**Sightseeing Only.** If your choice for visiting the park is to visit the overlooks, I recommend taking the short walk from the Visitor Center to the paved trail to Bright Angel Point, which provides a spectacular view of the canyon. You can see and hear Roaring Springs more than 3,000 feet below. Point Imperial is located 11 miles from the Visitor Center and is the highest point of the Grand Canyon. Cape Royal is the final stop and is located 14 miles from the junction of Point Imperial and Cape Royal. Take the short self-guided nature trail to Angels Window Overlook.

*North Rim Lodge*

*Snow Canyon State Park, Utah*

**Hiking Trail Recommendations.** Hiking options at the North Rim are unlimited. My recommendations for hiking are as follows:

- Bright Angel Point Trail (easy): .5 mile
- Uncle Jim Trail (moderate): 5 miles
- Widforss Trail (moderate): 10 miles
- Ken Patrick Trail (moderate): 20 miles
- North Kaibab Trail to Roaring Springs (strenuous): 9.4 miles
- North Kaibab Trail to Bright Angel Campground (strenuous): 28 miles

# Great Areas to Visit Within 60 Miles of Zion

**Coral Pink Sand Dunes State Park.** Located 12 miles of U.S. Highway 89 between Zion and Kanab, http://parks.state.ut.us, 435-648-2800, P.O. Box 95, Kanab, UT 84741. Unique coral-pink sand dunes, hiking, ATVs, and photography, plus a 22-unit campground and showers.

**The Johnson's Farm Dinosaur Tracks.** www.dino trax.com, 435-634-5747, 2000 East Riverside Drive, St. George, UT 84790. Recently discovered dinosaur tracks are probably the best ever found. Consist of two dinosaurs: the Dilophosaurus and the Coelophysis.

**Shakespearean Festival.** www.bard.com, 800-752-9849, 435-586-7878, Southern Utah University, 315 W. Center Street, Cedar City, UT. Tony-award-winning productions of Shakespeare and other plays. June–Sept.

**Snow Canyon State Park.** http://parks.state.ut.us, 435-628-2255, located 9 miles north of St. George along Highway 18. P.O. Box 140, Santa Clara, UT 84765. Unique geologic features of sandstone and volcanic rock. Hikes, climbing, sand dunes, camping.

**Tuacahn Amphitheatre.** www.showutah.com , 800-SHOWUTAH, 435-652-3300, Ivans, UT (near St. George). Outdoor theater productions in a beautiful canyon surrounded by 1,500 feet of cliffs.

# 10. So, What is It?: Common Questions about Zion Canyon

In no other place on earth can you find the intense beauty and natural wonders that Zion has to offer. The powerful and dramatic landscapes provide unique geological features, plant and animal life, and wonderment that can keep the mind occupied with the questions. *How did this all come about? What lies within this magic canyon? What plants and animals call this place home?* The natural history of Zion spans millions of years and begins with an amazing geologic creation.

Many visitors to this area are fascinated with Zion's natural history and mention should be given to the many inquiries visitors have regarding specific features found in the park. Here are the answers to the most commonly asked questions:

### What's an arch?

There are actually two types of arches; the natural or true arch and the blind arch. Both are natural arch-shaped rock structures formed when the rock erodes or falls out from underneath them. A true arch can be walked under and a blind arch is formed on the face of a cliff with no passage through it.

### What's the difference between an arch and a natural bridge?

A natural bridge has or did have water running underneath it, eroding a pathway through the solid rock, creating the bridge.

### How is an arch made?

Arches are formed when erosion of the underlying support reaches a point where the "potential arch area" is left as an overhang. Under its own sheer weight the rock begins to sag in the center, pulling from both sides, causing a fracture line perpendicular to the closest underlying support. The fracture then travels the path of least resistance (the shape of an arch), until it finally breaks loose and the rock comes crashing down, leaving behind a newly formed arch.

*Kolob Arch*

### How was Checkerboard Mesa formed?

The checkerboard pattern is a result of two separate processes. The horizontal lines were created when the sand dune was being formed. Windblown sands stacked one layer on top of the other. The vertical lines were created due to expansion of the sandstone surface. Sandstone contains water and will expand during cold weather. Checkerboard Mesa is located at an elevation that allows this to happen. As the stone expanded it was unable to stretch. With equal pressure being placed throughout the mesa, the fractures occurred in what appear to be very symmetrical lines.

### What causes the different pattern lines on the rock?

This is a process called cross-bedding. When windblown sands form a dune, the sands pile up at an angle or on a slope. As the dune becomes larger, it begins to act as a wind block and forces the wind direction to change. The sand is then redirected and begins piling up in a different location. The different line patterns are representative of this process.

## What is desert crust?

Known as cryptobiotic crust, this wonderful feature is found in soils and is dominated by the cyanobacteria. These soils play an important role in the ecosystem by preventing soil erosion and converting unusable nitrogen from the air to usable nitrogen for surrounding plants. The cyanobacteria moves throughout the soil leaving behind a sticky, sheath-like substance that sticks to surface soils, creating an intricate web of fibers that join the soil particles together. Advanced colonies of this crust resemble a mini cityscape. Please don't bust the crust! Walk on established trails or in areas void of this wonderful addition to our deserts.

## What is the black, shiny stuff on the cliffs?

This is desert varnish and often colors entire mountains. Only about one hundredth of a millimeter thick, this remarkable biogeochemical phenomenon is formed by colonies of microscopic bacteria living on the rock surface for thousands of years. The bacteria absorb trace amounts of manganese and iron from the atmosphere and precipitate it as a black layer of manganese oxide. The shinier the surface, the older the colony. It is in desert varnish where you find petroglyphs.

## What are the green and orange crust on the rocks?

This is called lichen crust and can manifest itself in many colors. This is a remarkable symbiotic relationship between algae and fungus. There are literally hundreds of different species in the Southwest, including leafy forms and low-growing forms that resemble a thick coat of paint. The lichen are composed of algal cells living inside fungal tissue. The algae provide the fungus with carbohydrates and the fungus provides the algae with protection from the harsh elements. Neither could survive without the other.

## What causes the streaking on the walls?

Several different colors of streaking can be found on Zion's cliffs. Red streaking (as on the Altar of Sacrifice), which appears to be blood streaming down the wall, consists mostly of iron oxide being washed down over the cliff tops from the oxide-laden capping formation. The black streaking is the result of decomposing plant minerals that are washed over the edge.

The white streaks come from spring lines that have evaporated or are evaporating, leaving behind calcium carbonate.

## Why are the cliffs red?

Rocks are the result of many mineral-laden sediments that become compressed and cemented together over millions of years. One of the dominant minerals found in Zion is iron oxide. To put it simply, iron oxide is iron, and just as with a piece of iron exposed to the elements, it rusts. Our cliffs are rusting, giving them the beautiful red colors.

## What is the average cliff height?

Although many variations of cliff heights are found throughout the canyon, if one were to average them out, the average cliff height would be about 2,600 feet.

## What keeps the cliffs so vertical or sheer?

As you observe the cliffs, notice the vertical fractures or cracks throughout the sandstone. These fractures were caused when this area began lifting, over 15 million years ago. The cliffs remain vertical as a result of the erosion process of sandstone. The softer layer of the Kayenta formation, the formation on which the sandstone sits, erodes away at a faster rate than the sandstone above it. Once the Kayenta formation has eroded out from beneath the sandstone back to one of the fracture lines, there is nothing left to support the massive rock or cliff and it comes crashing down.

## Where does the water come from that we see in places like Weeping Rock, Emerald Pools, or other seeps along the trails?

The water comes from within the sandstone itself. Sandstone is very porous and contains a large amount of water. The water travels downward through the sandstone until it reaches an impervious layer of stone that forces the water out of the sandstone and down the sides where you are able to see it. When you see the water seeping or running out of the sandstone, it can be anywhere from 2,000 to 4,000 years old.

## What are flash floods?

Flash floods are the result of an introduction of sudden waters from rain or thunderstorms. When it rains, the cliffs shed water into the nearest drainage. When the rains are heavy, the drainages can fill with large amounts of water very quickly. Often drainages can become raging torrents of water in a very short time.

## What are the large white trumpet flowers?

This beautiful flower is the Sacred Datura (*Datura wrightii Regel*). The flowers are 5–8 inches long and equally wide. They bloom from early spring through autumn, and open during the late evening and remain in bloom all night long, closing during the day. Because they bloom at night, the nickname Moon Lily has been adopted. This plant is a member of the potato family and is poisonous. *Do not eat it.*

## Where do I find hanging gardens?

Hanging gardens, a term used for vegetation growing (or hanging) on the cliff faces, can be found anywhere we have water seepage. The most common of the gardens containing plants such as golden columbine, cliff columbine, blue shooting stars, orange monkeyflowers, and maidenhair fern are the Riverside Walk, Weeping Rock, and Lower Emerald Pools.

## What type of tree is along the river?

The most common tree is the Fremont cottonwood.

## When do the flowers bloom?

This is probably one of the most difficult questions to answer. Each year, the unique combination of sun, wind, water, and temperature sets the stage for bloom times. Typical blooming times are from late February through early summer and again in early fall after the summer rains in August.

*Emerald Pools*

## What is the best time to see fall colors?

Because of the different elevations found in the park, the changing fall colors will begin in September at the higher elevations and continue through November in the lower areas. The best guess for seeing the fall colors in Zion's main canyon would be sometime in mid-October.

## What is the large black bird flying around the canyon?

This bird is the common raven, 22–27 inches long, large and all black, with a wedge-shaped tail, and long wings with feathers that spread out like fingers during flight. Ravens are primarily scavengers.

## Did I see a wild turkey?

Yes, Zion is home to many wild turkeys. Often you will find them near the Court of the Patriarchs, Zion Lodge, or anywhere along the scenic drive. The turkeys are doing very well and will roost in the trees at night. Keep an eye out for them early in the morning as they fly down from their roosting spots.

## Are there wolves in the park?

No, the wolves were eradicated from this area in the late 1800s and were never reintroduced. A close cousin of the wolf, the coyote, does live here and can often be seen throughout the canyon area. Listen to the sounds of the coyote just after sundown.

## Are there rattlesnakes in the park?

Yes, the most common of the rattlesnakes is the Mohave rattler and can be found just about anywhere. Rattlesnakes are very timid animals and pose little threat if left alone. If you encounter a rattlesnake suddenly, freeze in your tracks. Then, without turning your back, move away very slowly. The snake may not be able to see you well enough to strike if you don't make any sudden moves.

## What kind of lizard has the bright blue tail?

There are actually two different lizards that will sport the blue tail—the skink and also the whiptail. Watch for them along the trails and on the rocks.

## What type of squirrels are we seeing?

Although there are five different squirrels known to be in the park, the white-tailed antelope squirrel, the golden-mantled ground squirrel, the rock squirrel, red squirrel, and the Northern flying squirrel the most common found is the rock squirrel. Listen for the rock squirrel as you're hiking; it will chirp like a bird.

### Is that a mule deer that we see?

Yes, the mule deer is found throughout the park and is recognized by (and named for) the large mule-looking ears. The deer use the large ears to help cool their bodies by dissipating body heat.

### What is the large yellow and black butterfly we see?

That is the two-tailed tiger swallowtail. This butterfly can be found throughout the park.

### Are there mountain lions in the park?

Zion is home to a healthy population of mountain lions. This beautiful and graceful creature can be found just about anywhere within the park boundaries. Its diet consists mostly of deer but it will eat almost any type of animal it can catch if hungry. The mountain lion (also called a cougar) is typically very timid toward humans and a chance encounter is very unlikely.

### Are there bears in the park?

For the most part the answer is no. On occasion in the high elevation of the backcountry, there have been bear sightings. This is so rare that, generally speaking, this is not bear country.

### Are there any fish in the river?

The Virgin River does have fish in it, including the speckled dace, desert sucker, flannelmouth sucker, brown trout, cutthroat trout, and rainbow trout. Fishing is permitted with a Utah fishing license; however the fishing is reportedly not very good.

### Is it okay to remove some of the rocks or other items we find from the park?

No, federal law prohibits removing anything from a national park and with good reason. Imagine you find a really nice example of a fossil and remove it from the park—no big deal, right? Now imagine that 3 million visitors a year remove a really nice fossil from the park! It was fun for you to find, so we ask that you leave it so that someone else can have fun finding it.

If your question wasn't answered here, ask at the Visitor Center.

*Emerald Pools*

# 11. Geology: Simple Explanations

Everybody is familiar with our Earth, but very few understand the complexity of the Earth's formation. Zion is but a small portion of the overall Earth surface, but by understanding the basic principles of geology, you will be better able to understand the fantastic geologic story of Zion. What follows are simple explanations to basic geological principles.

## What is Geology?

Geology is the study of the origin, structure, and history of the earth and its inhabitants as recorded in the rocks. The science of geology is complex and oftentimes difficult to understand.

### The Age of the Earth

The formation of Zion and the continual process that shapes this beautiful canyon are the same processes that shaped the Earth from its beginning, some 4.5 billion years ago.

### Composition of the Earth

The Earth consists of air, water, and land. The Earth is, for the most part, round with a slight flattening at the poles and a slight bulge along the equator. The Earth's diameter is approximately 7,900 miles with a circumference of 24,874 miles and a surface area of about 197 million square miles. Of the total surface area, water covers about 71 percent with landmass covering only 29 percent.

## Geologic Forces

The Earth goes through many changes over long periods of time; those changes are the result of the several geologic forces including erosion, plate tectonic movement, and volcanism.

## Erosion

The surface rocks of the Earth are constantly being changed as a result of erosion. With the continual attacks by our atmosphere we see chemical and physical changes causing weathering, as well as rivers, lakes, and oceans wearing away rock fragments, transporting them to different locations as deposition.

## Plate-Tectonic Movement

According to accepted plate-tectonic theory, it is believed that the Earth's surface is broken into a number of plates, which average about 50 miles in thickness. Upon these plates ride the different continents of Earth, including the ocean continents. When these plates move as a result of deep Earth pressure, the continents change geographic location (or drift) and dramatic surface changes may occur. The collision of these plates results in buckling (mountains), separation (basins), or uplifting (plateaus).

## Volcanism

Referring to the movement of molten rock from deep within the Earth's surface. Volcanic processes produce lava flows, ash, cinders, and volcanoes. This process is also responsible for the rocks known as igneous rocks, or the rocks formed as the molten rock cools at a great depth within the Earth.

# What Makes a Rock?

There are basically three kinds of rock: igneous, sedimentary, and metamorphic. Each are formed differently, however all may become one or the other. To put it simply, our landmasses are a result of the earth recycling itself. Igneous rocks become sedimentary rocks, which can become metamorphic rocks, which can become igneous or sedimentary rocks. A continual process of erosion, plate-tectonic movement, and volcanism change the rocks' composition. To better

understand the different rocks and their makeup the following definitions are offered:

## Igneous Rocks

Rocks that have solidified from an original molten state. The most commonly known igneous rock is lava or basalt. Most igneous rock is brought to the Earth's surface by volcanoes. Other igneous rock may be forced into cracks or in some other manner be forced into existing rocks. Igneous rocks can be identified by the texture, structure, mineral content, and the complete lack of fossils.

## Sedimentary Rock

These rocks are commonly known as sandstone, shale, and limestone, and make up about 75 percent of all the exposed rock found on the Earth's surface. Sedimentary rocks are formed when any of the three mentioned rock types experience erosion. The fragments of eroding rock are transported, laid down, re-cemented and compressed into a new rock formations (known as sedimentation or sedimentary deposition). Cementing agents used to join rock fragments are the minerals, or chemical elements found naturally within the Earth's crust. Sedimentary rocks are a mixture of rock fragments and cementing minerals

*Ron and his rocks*

(a process known as lithification). Certain minerals, such as calcite, quartz, and feldspar, are so commonly found in rocks that they are called the rock-forming minerals.

### Metamorphic Rock

These rocks are formed when former sedimentary or igneous rocks have been buried deep within the Earth and are subjected to high temperatures and pressures. The rock changes or metamorphoses into a new rock. Marble is a good example of this change.

### Soil Formation

Soil is simply eroded rock fragments that have not yet been cemented together.

# What is a Mountain?

Mountains are regions of high elevation that rise conspicuously above the surrounding area. A "mountain range" is formed when a series of mountains are grouped together. Mountains may originate as a result of plate-tectonic plate movement or as a result of igneous rock movement via a volcano or fracture intrusion. Tectonic-involved mountains result when the Earth's crust is literally folded and pushed up as a result of plate movement or collision between two plates. This process is similar to the bent and folded metal on an automobile after a collision. Igneous mountain formation results from volcanic activity, forming a cinder cone or volcano. The most well-known igneous formed mountains are Mount Hood, Mount St. Helens, and Mount Ranier in Washington state.

# What is a Plateau?

Plateaus are large, essentially level, masses of land of considerable size and elevation, which consist of horizontal rock formations. Their surfaces are typically trenched with canyons and gorges. Most plateaus are more than 2,000 feet above sea level. Some, like the Colorado Plateau, are more than 1 mile above sea level. Plateaus result from uplift, usually as a result of tectonic plate movement.

Mention should be given to other features that rise conspicuously above the surrounding countryside. These formations, unlike mountains and plateaus, are not the result of movement deforming or disturbing the rocks; they are simply the remnants of highlands that are in various stages of erosion.

### What is a Mesa?

Mesa, Spanish for flat or table, is a large flat-topped hill longer than it is tall.

### What is a Butte?

A butte is a mesa that is more advanced in its erosion and usually as tall as it is wide.

### What is a Spire?

A spire is the final result of the butte erosion. Needle-like in appearance, it is defined as taller than it is wide.

To put the process simply, a mesa becomes a butte, a butte becomes a spire, and the spire finally disappears.

# Conclusion

What does the geologist learn from studying rocks? He or she learns what was happening to this planet millions of years ago. He or she knows that the Earth and its inhabitants have gone through many changes during the life span of our planet. He or she knows what processes have occurred in order to create an area as beautiful as Zion National Park.

# 12. Prominent Feature Place Names

Zion National Park is known for its majestic peaks, towering cliffs, and spectacular scenery. For years people have been coming to Zion and discovering places like Angels Landing, The Great White Throne, Altar of Sacrifice, and other prominent features throughout the park. But how did these features get their names? Reverend Frederick Fisher, an early explorer of the park, as well as many other early settlers, explorers, and Native Americans, named many of the prominent features. The following is a list of some of the most popular features and how they got their name.

**Altar of Sacrifice (7,410 ft.)** Located among the Temples of the Virgin, west of the administration building, is the Altar of Sacrifice. Red iron oxide streaking down its face gives the appearance of blood on a sacrificial altar. Clarence Dutton may have named it.

**Angels Landing (5,785 ft.)** Reverend Frederick Fisher, Vining Fisher, Ethelbert Bingham, and Claud Hirschi were exploring Zion in 1916. While looking at the prominent peak Bingham suggested that "only an angel could land on it." All agreed. Later the area was visited by Utah Governor Spry and other dignitaries who stated that many of the features in Zion were similar to Yosemite's "El Capitan." Someone suggested that Angels Landing or the Great White Throne be renamed "El Gobernador" in honor of Governor Spry, who had been instrumental in getting early funding for Zion. In the end, the original names given by Reverend Fisher to the two peaks became the official names.

**Beartrap Canyon** A canyon draining west into La Verkin Creek believed to be named because a pioneer cornered a wounded bear there.

**Beatty Point (7,770 ft.)** A west-jutting ridge above the south fork of Taylor Creek was named for the Beatty family of Toquerville.

**Beehives (6,825 ft.)** Beehive-shaped peaks located northwest of the administration building. The beehive is the Utah state symbol. Origin of the name is unknown.

*Angels Landing*

**Behunin Canyon** A small canyon west of Mt. Majestic that drains south into Heaps Canyon near the Lower Emerald Pools. Named for Isaac Behunin, the first settler in the canyon with a farm near the present-day lodge.

**Big Springs** The largest springs located on the west wall of the Zion Canyon Narrows just before entering the narrowest part of the canyon from the north side.

**Birch Creek** A stream that flows eastward below the Court of the Patriarchs into the Virgin River. Named for the water birch trees growing in that area.

**The Bishopric (7,021 ft., 7,251 ft., and 7,327 ft.)** Three white peaks at the head of Jennings Wash.

Originally named Councilor Peaks in 1934, by R. T. Evans, a topographic engineer with the U.S. Geological Survey, to honor the organization of the bishop and two councilors of each unit of the Mormon Church. The name was later changed to the Bishopric, which is inclusive of the councilors.

**Black's Canyon** A canyon that drains southeast from the West Temple into the Virgin River. Named for Joseph Black, an early pioneer of Springdale and possibly the second white man to enter Zion Canyon.

**Blue Creek** A stream that begins above Blue Springs Reservoir near Lava Point and flows down Wildcat Canyon into the Left Fork of North Creek.

**Bridge Mountain (6,814 ft.)** East of the Zion Canyon administration building, this peak was originally called Crawford Mountain in honor of the William Crawford family, pioneers who had a farm near the current administration building. The name changed to Bridge Mountain when Mrs. Crawford noticed the natural arch (or bridge, as the pioneers called it) near the peak.

**Buck Pasture Mountain (8,035 ft.)** Located at the head of the south fork of Taylor Creek, Buck Pasture Mountain is believed to be named for the pioneer sheepman's buck pasture.

**Bull Pen Mountain (7,100 ft.)** Located east of La Verkin Creek; named for a pioneer bull pasture.

**Burnt Mountain (7,669 ft.)** Located west of Hop Valley. There are two possible reasons for the name—a fire burned the top many years ago and it is also said that the late afternoon sun makes it appear to be on fire.

**Cable Mountain (6,469 ft.)** Located east of Weeping Rock; named for the pioneer cable works, in operation from 1900 to 1926, that brought lumber down from the mesa on a 3,300-foot cable to the present-day site of the Weeping Rock parking lot.

**Cane Creek** Located south of Stapely Point; flows west into Currant Creek in the Kolob Canyons Area.

**Castle Dome (6,819 ft.)** Located northwest of the Emerald Pools. Named by Stephen S. Johnson, a lecturer and real estate salesman from New Jersey in 1922 because it resembles the dome of a castle.

**Cathedral Mountain (6,900 ft.)** Located west of Angels Landing; named by Stephen S. Johnson in 1922 because the formations at the top resemble a cathedral.

**Cave Canyon** Located north of the east entrance station and running southwest from Clear Creek Mountain into Zion Canyon. Named for the cave formations within the canyon.

**Cave Knoll (6,518 ft.)** Located between Cave Valley and Lee Valley; named for some small caves at its base.

**Checkerboard Mesa (6,670 ft.)** Located near the east entrance; originally named Checkerboard Mountain by Preston P. Patraw, the third superintendent of Zion National Park. Named for its checkerboard pattern caused by the horizontal cross-bedding of ancient sand dunes and vertical cracking due to expansion and contraction of the sandstone.

**Clear Creek** Located at the eastern boundary of the park and flows west to the head of Pine Creek near the East Tunnel entrance.

**Coalpits Wash** A large, usually dry wash that runs south through the southwestern corner of the park. Named for the black lava rock that looks like coal and borders it on the west.

**Corral Hollow** A canyon located on Horse Pasture Plateau that drains southeast into the Virgin River Narrows at Big Springs. Named for a pioneer horse corral that was located there.

**Cougar Mountain (6,479 ft.)** Located between North Creek and Coalpits Wash; named for the large number of mountain lions, or cougars, that inhabit it.

**Crater Hill (5,207 ft.)** A cinder cone located in the southwest corner of the park.

**Crawford Wash** A canyon located between Parunuweap Canyon and Clear Creek running south. Named by the Park Service to honor William R. Crawford, the first bishop of Springdale and an early farmer/pioneer in the area where the Nature Center is now.

**Currant Creek** Located in the southwestern corner of the Kolob Canyons section. It flows west into La Verkin Creek and drains the west face of Burnt Mountain. Named for the wild currants growing there.

**Death Point (7,559 ft.)** A high mesa located north of La Verkin Creek; named because an early settler lost a band of sheep there when early snows trapped them.

**Deep Creek** Located near the northern boundary of the park and flows south through a deep, narrow canyon into the north fork of the Virgin River.

**Deertrap Mountain (6,882 ft.)** Located across from the Court of the Patriarchs, this narrow mesa juts out from the east rim. It got its name because the Paiute Indians drove mule deer onto the mesa, then trapped and killed them.

**Dennett Canyon** Located east of Transview Mountain and runs north into Parunuweap Canyon. Named by the Park Service to honor Dave Dennett, a Springdale stockman and the first regularly employed horseback guide in Zion Canyon.

**East Temple (7,110 ft.)** Located on the north side of Pine Creek; John Wesley Powell named this giant monolith.

**Echo Canyon** Located between Observation Point and Cable Mountain from the Weeping Rock trailhead, it received its name because of the distinct echo.

**Emerald Pools** Four pools: an upper, two middle, and one lower pool, located in Heaps Canyon across from the Zion Lodge. Named for the emerald green algae growing in them.

**Firepit Knoll (7,274 ft.)** Located north of the Kolob Terrace road, the name was given to this cinder cone because of volcanic activity.

**Gifford Canyon** Located between Parunuweap Canyon and Pine Creek near the east tunnel entrance. Named for Oliver Gifford, early pioneer and bishop of Springdale.

**Goose Creek** Located just above Big Springs in the Virgin River Narrows flowing from near Lava Point. The name origin is unknown.

**Grapevine Wash** A wash that drains Cave Valley into the lower end of the Left Fork of North Creek; named for the wild grapevines growing along it.

**Great Arch of Zion** Located up the switchbacks to Zion Tunnel, this blind arch is 720 feet long, 580 feet high, and 90 feet deep; one stands on top of it at the end of the Canyon Overlook Trail.

**Greatheart Mesa (7,410 ft.)** Located between the left fork of North Creek and Wildcat Canyon, this white-walled mesa was named in 1934 by R. T. Evans, topographic engineer for the U.S. Geological Survey, for the Christians' guide in *Pilgrim's Progress* Evans felt "to attain the summit of this grand mesa will require a staunch heart and an arduous, sustained effort, and the candidate should have the best guide obtainable."

**Great West Canyon** Located at the beginning of Wildcat Canyon, flowing southwest toward the town of Virgin, it is the drainage for the Right Fork of North Creek.

**Great White Throne (6,744 ft.)** Located on the east side of Zion Canyon, north of the lodge, this enormous white sandstone monolith was named by Reverend Frederick Fisher in 1916. On a return trip from the Temple of Sinawava, Reverend Fisher and his companions had stopped to take a picture when one young companion fell into the river. Fisher fished him out, and after they had composed themselves, one of the companions asked, "What is that?" Fisher turned and looked directly at the giant rock, then said, "Well boys, there is only one name for that. I have been looking for it all my life. I never expected to find it in America or on the earth itself. That is the GREAT WHITE THRONE!" Thus, the Great White Throne was given its name, in reference to the Throne of God, with white being its principal color. When viewed from the Big Bend viewpoint, it resembles the back of a gigantic throne with Angels Landing as its left armrest and the Organ as the armrest on its right.

**Gregory Butte (7,705 ft.)** Located in the Kolob Canyons section, this peak was given its name in honor of Herbert E. Gregory, a famous geologist who did much scientific research in the park.

**The Grotto** Located north of the Zion Lodge, now a picnic area. This location in the 1920s was once the park's northernmost campground, and the road ended at that point. The Park Service gave it its name.

**Guardian Angels (7,408 ft., 7,165 ft.)** Located on the west side of the park, the North Guardian and the

South Guardian Angel are two prominent, pointed sandstone peaks believed to be guardians of the park. Exact name origin is unknown.

**Heaps Canyon** Located across from the Zion Lodge running east into Zion Canyon, this canyon was named in honor of William Heap, who had a cabin and farm near the river on the north side of the creek below the Lower Emerald Pool. He and his family moved there in 1863, becoming the second family to move into Zion Canyon.

**Hepworth Wash** A tributary of Pine Creek located in the high country above Parunuweap Canyon, it spills into Pine Creek across the face of window #6 in the tunnel. Named by the Park Service in honor of Thornton Hepworth, early resident in Springdale.

**Herb Point (7,302 ft.)** Located between Death Point and Bull Pen Mountain in the Kolob Section. Origin of name unknown.

**Hidden Canyon** Located on the east side of the Great White Throne and runs north. First explored in 1927 when W. H. Evans, a mountain climber who was the first man to climb the Great White Throne, fell in his descent and was seriously injured. Rescue was made through Hidden Canyon, which was so named because it cannot be seen from the canyon floor.

**Hop Valley** Located 12.5 miles from Virgin, up the Kolob Terrace, Hop Valley was formed by a drainage that runs north into La Verkin Creek below the Kolob Arch. Named because of the wild hops that used to grow there.

**Horse Pasture Plateau (7,300 ft.)** Located near Lava Point and running south, the West Rim Trail runs the length of this plateau. Named for the beautiful pastures located there where pioneers used to range their horses.

**Horse Ranch Mountain (8,726 ft.)** Located in the northern part of the Kolob section, this is the highest point in Zion. Believed to be named for the pioneer horse ranches there.

**Huber Wash** Located in the southwest corner of the park running south to the Virgin River; named for the Huber family.

**Imlay Canyon** Located on the West Rim and runs southwest from Potato Hollow into the Virgin River Narrows. Named for a pioneer family of the area.

**Inclined Temple (7,156 ft.)** Located between Phantom Valley and the Right Fork of North Creek. Named because it appears to be leaning.

**Ivins Mountain (7,019 ft.)** Located at the headwaters of the Right Fork of North Creek near the Inclined Temple; named by the Park Service to honor Anthony W. Ivins, early-day stockman and pioneer, Mormon apostle, and one of the earliest promoters of Zion as a place worthy of National Park status.

**Jennings Wash** Runs southwest from the Bishopric into Coalpits Wash; named by the Park Service to honor Henry Jennings, who settled in Rockville in the fall of 1862.

**Jobs Head (7,902 ft.)** Located on the southeast end of Hop Valley, this high promontory point's name of origin is unknown.

**Johnson Mountain (6,153 ft.)** Located south of the Watchman; named in honor of Nephi Johnson, the first white explorer to enter Zion Canyon.

**Jolley Gulch** Located near the east entrance and connects with Clear Creek; named for a pioneer family that settled near Mt. Carmel.

**Kolob** The northwest section of Zion. It is not known who named the area "Kolob" but the earliest pioneer journals record that name for it. The first exploration party into the area, led by Parley P. Pratt in 1851, probably named it. *Kolob*, in Mormon theology, is the first creation, greatest of the governing stars of the universe, and is located nearest to the residence of God (see Abraham 3:2–10 and Facsimile No. 2, *Pearl of Great Price*).

**Kolob Arch** Located near Gregory Butte and north of La Verkin Creek. This arch is believed to be one of the largest freestanding arches in the world with a span of 310 feet.

**Kolob Creek** Located above Kolob Reservoir and running southeast past Lava Point, entering the Virgin River Narrows between Deep Creek and Goose Creek.

**Lady Mountain (6,945 ft.)** Located on the west side of Zion Canyon across from Zion Lodge; named because early pioneers claimed to see the figure of a lady in its sheer north face. People began to climb it in the late 1910s and early 1920s, even before a trail was built to its top. Some of them started an organization called "Mount Zion Mountaineers," headquartered in Chicago, Illinois, and lobbied to have its name changed to Mount Zion. Eivind T. Scoyen, first superintendent of Zion, joined them in their efforts. Some of the park materials in the late 1920s even listed it as Mount Zion. The name that was officially adopted, however, was Lady Mountain.

**Langston Canyon** Running south from Langston Mountain into Hop Valley, this canyon was named for the Langston family, early pioneers in Rockville.

**Langston Mountain (7,453 ft.)** Located between Beartrap Canyon and Hop Valley, this mountain was named after the Langston family of Rockville.

**Lava Point (7,980 ft.)** Located off the Kolob Terrace Road, Lava Point is the highest point in the park that one can drive; named for the lava flows of the area.

**La Verkin Creek** A drainage of the Kolob section of Zion that flows into the town of La Verkin; believed to have received its name from a corruption of the Spanish phrase *La Virgen*, meaning the Virgin, in honor of the Virgin Mary.

**Lee Pass** A high point on the Kolob Canyons Road where John D. Lee, one of the earliest pioneer explorers, and one of the first settlers in the area, hid out from Federal authorities when he found himself in trouble in the 1860s because of his role in the Mountain Meadows Massacre.

**Lee Valley** Located on the lower Kolob Plateau just above Smith Mesa; named in honor of some of John D. Lee's descendants who homesteaded, lived, and farmed there.

**Little Creek** Located at Little Creek Peak southwest of Kolob Reservoir outside of the park. It flows south to the Little Creek sinks just inside the park boundary, continues on southward around the west side of Pocket Mesa into Pine Valley, and on into the left fork of North Creek, at a point just east of where Pine Valley Wash enters the left fork. Presumably named because of the small amount of water in it.

**Long Point** A long, narrow ridge that runs south from Langston Mountain toward Hop Valley ending in a point, probably named because of its length.

**Meridian Tower (7,309 ft.)** Located north of the Altar of Sacrifice on the 113th Meridian within the Towers of the Virgin, which were collectively named by Clarence Dutton.

**Moquitch Hill** Located between Springdale and the Obert C. Tanner Amphitheatre. The name is derived from a Paiute Indian tradition that it was a campsite of the Moqui Indians, locally pronounced "Moquitch."

**Mountain of Mystery (6,545 ft.)** Located east of the Narrows and south of Orderville Canyon; named because Mystery Falls originates below it.

**Mountain of the Sun (6,723 ft.)** Located on the east side of Zion Canyon just south of Zion Lodge; named by William W. Wylie, who constructed the "Wylie Way Camp" in 1917. The mountain was so named because it is the first place from that site on which the sun can be seen shining in the mornings and the last place on which it can be seen shining at night.

**Mount Kinesava (7,276 ft.)** Located on the southwest end of Zion Canyon, visible as one enters the park from Rockville; named for "Kinesava," the Paiute god who controlled the actions of the deer according to his moods, rolled rocks off the high cliff walls when he felt like pulling pranks, and lit fires high upon inaccessible places like the face of the Great White Throne or the West Temple. The Paiutes thought Kinesava used the fires to send smoke signals to their enemies, the Navajos, informing them of the Paiutes' location.

**Mount Majestic (6,951 ft.)** Located north of the Emerald Pools; named by Stephen S. Johnson on a trip up the canyon in the company of Oliver and Freeborn Gifford, Walter Ruesch, and Harold Russell in 1922.

**Mount Moroni (5,667 ft.)** Located below and in front of the Three Patriarchs; named in honor of

Moroni, one of the principal figures in *The Book of Mormon*.

**Mount Spry (5,823 ft.)** Located between the Virgin River and the East Temple; named by the Park Service in 1934 to honor William Spry, ex-governor of Utah.

**Mukuntuweap** The name originally given to Zion in 1909 when part of this area was designated Mukuntuweap National Monument, a Paiute Indian word meaning straight, narrow canyon.

**Mystery Falls** Located in the Virgin River Narrows about .5 mile from the end of the Riverside Walk; named because its source was inaccessible.

**Nagunt Mesa (7,803 ft.)** Located between Timber Top and Buck Pasture Mountains in Kolob, this triangular mesa possibly got its name from the Paiute word *Naga*, meaning bighorn sheep.

**The Narrows** A narrow canyon with the North Fork of the Virgin River flowing down its walls. Named by Grove K. Gilbert of Captain George M. Wheeler's 1872 expedition to map areas of southern Utah. He is thought to be the first white man to explore it and made the statement, "the narrows . . . the most wonderful defile it has been my fortune to behold."

**Neagle Ridge (6,750 ft.)** Juts off Burnt Mountain between Hop Valley and La Verkin Creek; named for a pioneer family of the Toquerville area.

**Northgate Peaks (7,267 ft., 7,250 ft., 6,812 ft.)** Located just north of the North Guardian Angel, the name of these three peaks' origin is unknown.

**Oak Creek** This stream runs east from the West Temple area into the Virgin River; named because of the Gambel Oaks and shrub oaks that grow along its banks.

**Observation Point (6,508 ft.)** This is a lookout located on Mount Baldy; named by Stephen S. Johnson in 1922 when it was a long circuitous, 18-mile round-trip hike up to it. The switchbacks leading from Echo Canyon were not built until 1928.

**Orderville Canyon** Located from the east boundary of the park running west into the Virgin River Narrows. The canyon takes its name from the town of Orderville, which lies about 10 miles to the east. The name was derived from the fact that the Mormon settlers of that town lived, for about 10 years as the United Order, whereby everything was given to the Church and then allotted back to each individual according to need.

**The Organ (5,100 ft..)** A projecting rock formation connected to Angels Landing on the west by a jutting, low-level ridge; named by Reverend Fisher because of its resemblance to a pipe organ and the sound of the wind that could be heard there.

**Paria Point (7,000 ft..)** Located between the middle and south forks of Taylor Creek in the Kolob Section; named for the elk that inhabited the area. *Paria* means elk in Paiute.

**Parunuweap Canyon** The east fork of the Virgin River flows through this canyon from Mt. Carmel Junction; named because it is a narrow canyon through which water rushes during rains and flash floods. *Parunuweap* means "a place of rushing or roaring waters" in Paiute. The name was first recorded by John Wesley Powell as the name by which the Paiutes referred to the canyon.

**Petrified Forest** Located in the southwestern end of Zion and associated with the Chinle Trail. Named for the ancient forest, now petrified.

**Petty Point (elevation 4,600 ft..)** Located at the end of a spur extending southeast from the Three Marys. The name was given in honor of Albert Petty, founder and first resident of Springdale, Utah.

**Phantom Valley** An isolated valley that is very difficult to get to located between Horse Pasture Plateau and the Inclined Temple.

**Pine Creek** The drainage on the east side of Deertrap Mountain flowing in a southerly direction until it reaches Clear Creek at the Zion–Mt. Carmel Highway at which point it turns west and drains into Zion Canyon; named for the ponderosa and pinyon pines growing along it.

**Pine Valley** Located between Pocket Mesa and Northgate Peaks. Little Creek enters it on the north and flows out of it on the south; named for the pine growing there.

**Pine Valley Peak (7,428 ft..)** Located due west of Pine Valley.

**Pine Valley Wash** Located west of Blue Springs and drains down through Lee Valley west of Pine Valley Peak. Empties into the Left Fork of North Creek just west of Little Creek.

**Pocket Mesa (7,500 ft..)** Located between Russell Gulch and Pine Valley; origin of the name is unknown.

**Potato Hollow** Located along the West Rim Trail about halfway between West Rim Spring and Lava Point, it is a valley with springs and a southeast-flowing stream that drains into Imlay Canyon; named because of the many *koosharem* or Indian potatoes that grow there.

**The Pulpit** Located at the Temple of Sinawava, a large jutting rock that resembles a minister's pulpit; named by Reverend Fisher.

**Red Arch Mountain (5,924 ft..)** Located between the Great White Throne and Deertrap Mountain, a red sandstone peak with an enormous blind arch that formed in the early 1880s. May have conceivably been called Gifford Mountain prior to the massive rockfall that formed the arch because Oliver D. Gifford had a cornfield below it, which along with the spring he was using for irrigation, were covered by the collapse, forcing him to move his farm to Springdale. Named Red Arch Mountain in 1922 by Stephen S. Johnson.

**Refrigerator Canyon** Located along the West Rim Trail and runs south between Cathedral Mountain and Angels Landing. Named because it's very narrow and gets very little sunlight and thus stays cool all year.

**Russell Gulch** A tributary of North Creek that enters the left fork just east of the North Guardian Angel. Named by R. T. Evans, a topographic engineer with the U.S. Geological Survey, to honor Alonzo Havington Russell, who arrived in Grafton on November 10, 1861, and helped establish that community.

**Scoggins Wash** A tributary of Coalpits Wash that drains the high country below the Altar of Sacrifice in a southwesterly direction; named for the Scoggins family, early pioneers.

**Scout Lookout (5,300 ft.)** A viewpoint with a 1,000-foot sheer drop-off to the Virgin River overlooking Big Bend, located at the base of Angels Landing. It is believed to be named for scouts John and Barney Gifford, who first located and mapped a route for the West Rim trail.

**The Sentinel (7,157 ft.)** The northernmost peak of the Towers of the Virgin, located west of the administration building; named by Clarence Dutton of the U.S. Geological Survey in 1880. This imposing promontory appears to be a sentinel or guardian of Zion Canyon when viewed from upriver.

**Shunesburg Mountain (5,925 ft.)** Located at the confluence of Shunes Creek and Parunuweap Canyon; named because it is directly above and to the east of the ghost town of Shunesburg.

**Shunes Creek** The first pioneers to the area named the creek in honor of Shune or Shone, a Paiute brave who helped the settlers. The stream flows northwest into Parunuweap Canyon at the ghost town of Shunesburg.

**Shuntavi Butte (6,500 ft.)** Located west of Timbertop Mountain in the Kolob Canyons Section; may be a Paiute name, but its meaning and origin are unknown.

**Sleepy Hollow** Located along the West Rim trail between Potato Hollow and Telephone Canyon; drains into Imlay Canyon; origin of the name unknown.

**The Spearhead (5,857 ft.)** Located on the west side of the Virgin River just north of Zion Lodge. The massive sandstone cliff faces southeast and constitutes the lower reaches of Mount Majestic; named for its resemblance to a spearhead.

**Spendlove Knoll (6,893 ft.)** Located southwest of Firepit Knoll and east of Lee Valley; named for the Spendlove family, early settlers and farmers of the area.

**Stapely Point (6,000 ft.)** Located south of Burnt Mountain and west of Hop Valley, and separates the upper reaches of Cane and Current Creeks on the Kolob section. Named in honor of Charles Stapely, who was one of the first settlers in Toquerville and the first person to plant alfalfa in Utah's Dixie.

**Stevens Wash** A drainage south of Bridge Mountain to Parunuweap Canyon; origin of its name unknown.

**Streaked Wall (6,000 ft.)** Located on the west side of the Virgin River, this east-facing, massive, sheer cliff makes up the lower reaches of the Beehives. Named for the large amounts of mineral streaking on its face.

**Subway** Located in the upper reaches of the left fork of North Creek, this narrow canyon was given its name because the erosion pattern gives it the appearance of a subway tunnel and water rushing through it sounds like a subway train.

**The Sundial (7,438 ft.)** The southernmost peak of the Towers of the Virgin; named by the Park Service because the people of Grafton regulated their clocks by the early-morning sun hitting its peak.

**Tabernacle Dome (6,451 ft.)** A red sandstone butte between Grapevine and Pine Spring Washes just north of the lower end of the left fork of North Creek. Named because it resembles the dome of the Mormon Tabernacle in Salt Lake City.

**Taylor Creek** A stream with three forks (north, south, and middle) which flow down the finger canyons of Kolob; named for a pioneer family of the area who operated a sawmill there. It was historically called Dry Creek in the journals of John D. Lee.

**Telephone Canyon** A drainage southeast of the West Rim Trail on Horse Pasture Plateau, it enters Zion Canyon at the Falls of the Temple of Sinawava. Named because for many years the Park Service maintained a telephone line there between the Temple of Sinawava and Lava Point.

**Temple of Sinawava** A stadium-like area at the beginning of the Riverside Walk; named by Douglas White, a publicity agent for the Union Pacific Railroad, about 1913 to honor "Sinawava," the Paiute Wolf God or Good Spirit.

**Terry Wash** A southwesterly flowing tributary of Coalpits Wash, by way of Jennings Wash, that drains an area north and west of the Bishopric. Named by the Park Service to honor James Parshall Terry, one of the first settlers of Rockville between the years 1862 and 1896.

**Three Marys (6,364 ft., 6,118 ft., 5,916 ft.)** Three sandstone peaks located on the east face of the West Temple and east of the Bishopric; named by early pioneers to Springdale because "they felt such a name would be a tribute to the women who shared the hardships of the pioneers and who later did their full share of the work."

**Three Patriarchs (6,990 ft., 6,825 ft., 6,831 ft.)** Located on the west side of Zion Canyon at Birch Creek. The three peaks, Abraham, Isaac, and Jacob (the three ancient patriarchs of the Old Testament), were named by Reverend Fisher.

**Timbertop Mountain (8,075 ft.)** Located above and north of Kolob Arch; named for its heavy stands of conifer trees.

**Towers of the Virgin** The prominent peaks west of the administration building and north of the West Temple; named by Clarence Dutton of the U.S. Geological Survey as prominent towers of stone along the Virgin River.

**Trail Canyon** Drains north into the right fork of North Creek; named because pioneer cattlemen trailed their stock to and from the summer pastures near Cougar Mountain.

**Transview Mountain (6,315 ft.)** Located south of Parunuweap Canyon; originally called Transit Peak by R. T. Evans because it was a control station for some of the surveying of the Zion–Mt.Carmel Highway. The surveyors and engineers spent much time using transits there; name later changed to "Transview" by the Park Service.

**Tucupit Point (7,718 ft.)** Located between the north and middle forks of Taylor Creek in the Kolob section; named for the Paiute word for wildcat.

**Twin Brothers (6,850 ft.)** Located on the west side of Zion Canyon between the Mountain of the Sun and the East Temple; named because from Zion Canyon it appears to be two identical mountains but is actually a U-shaped peak that is joined on its east, out of sight of a viewer in the canyon.

**Virgin River** North fork begins north of Zion at Cascade Falls and the east fork originates above Long Valley, runs through the park, and empties into Lake

Mead. Named *La Virgen* by Spanish Catholics using a trail beside it that connected their missions in Santa Fe, New Mexico, and Los Angeles, California. *La Virgen* means The Virgin in honor of the Virgin Mary. However, the Spaniards named two rivers in the area, the Virgin and the Rio Severo, or Severe River (misspelled "Sevier"). The river that we know as the Virgin is a fast-falling, rapid river, subject to flash flooding, and can be very dangerous and destructive. On the other hand, the Sevier River, located just north of the Virgin, is a quiet, slowly meandering river that flows out into the Great Basin, never reaching the ocean. So, there is some argument that the names for the Virgin and the Sevier have actually been switched.

**Walter's Wiggles** Located about 2 miles from the Grotto picnic area along the West Rim Trail, there are 21 switchbacks that lead from the floor of Refrigerator Canyon to Scout Lookout. Named in honor of Walter Ruesch, first acting superintendent of Zion, who conceived of the idea of having the switchbacks and helped engineer and build them.

**The Watchman (6,555 ft.)** Located in the mouth of Zion Canyon on the east side above Springdale, originally called Flannigan's Peak by residents of Springdale. Some feel the name was later changed because someone saw the figure of a watchman in its sandstone pillars, but the most probable theory of the origin of its name is that it stands as a watchman over the beauties of Zion Canyon.

**Weeping Rock** Located near the end of the Scenic Drive, this alcove with water dripping from it was easily named because of this feature.

**West Temple (7,810 ft.)** Located west of the administrative offices, this cliff wall is the highest monolith in Zion Canyon. The Paiutes called it *Temp-o-i-tin-car-ur* or "mountain without a trail" because of its inaccessibility. The early Mormon settlers in the town of Virgin called it "Steamboat Mountain" because from that side it closely resembles a steamboat; Major John Wesley Powell, the second director of the U.S. Geological Survey, named it the West Temple when

he was exploring and mapping the Colorado River drainage areas.

**Wildcat Canyon** Located above Blue Springs Reservoir and following the Wildcat Canyon Fault along the entire west face of Horse Pasture Plateau, this canyon was named because of the mountain lions or wildcats that inhabit the area.

**Willis Creek** Beginning near Kolob Reservoir and flowing into Kolob Canyons, this creek joins La Verkin Creek at the base of Bull Pen Mountain north of Beartrap Canyon. Named for the Willis family, early settlers of Toquerville.

**Wylie's Retreat** or **Wylie Way Camp** Located at the sight of the current Zion Lodge, this was the first overnight accommodation in Zion. Built by William W. Wylie in 1917, the camp consisted of tentlike structures.

**Wynopits Mountain (6,891 ft.)** Located east of the Virgin River Narrows and north of Orderville Canyon; named in honor of one of the Paiute gods, or more closely, the Paiute devil or evil spirit, "Wynoptis."

**Zion** A Hebrew word that refers to a place of safety or refuge; a name given to the canyon by Isaac Behunin, the first white settler, who established a farm near where Zion Lodge is today. An old man when he settled in the canyon in 1862, he had been with the Mormons through all their persecutions, tribulations, and hardships. They, as a group, were searching for "Zion," a place where they could live in peace and practice their religion. Upon arriving in the canyon, Isaac Behunin could feel the peace and serenity of the area and, overwhelmed by its beauty, he stated, "I have found Zion—this is Zion!" He continued to call the canyon by that name and later when William Heap, John Rolfe, and their families moved into the canyon, an ecclesiastical unit of the Mormon Church was established with Mr. Heap acting as the presiding elder. The three families agreed that their community should continue to be called "Zion."

# 13. Surrounding Community Place Names

**Cedar City, UT** Originally called *Weseeapto*, a Paiute Indian word meaning "land of scrub cedars." In 1851 a group of settlers moved to the area after coal was discovered and named their new homestead Cedar City because of the juniper trees found there.

**Colorado City, AZ** Originally called Short Creek, this community changed their name in 1961 to Colorado City. Named for the Vermillion Cliffs in that area, *colorado*, in Spanish, means "reddish."

**Escalante, UT** The area near present-day Escalante was originally referred to as Potato Valley because of the wild potatoes found growing there during early exploration. In 1875 the township was established and named after the Escalante River flowing near there. The river had been named by members of the John Wesley Powell expeditionary party in honor of the Dominguez-Escalante expedition in 1776.

**Fredonia, AZ** Named from a contraction of the English word *Free* and the Spanish word *Dona* by an early Mormon leader referring to a free woman. The Mormons selected this name because of the practice of polygamy during early colonization. The site was selected to avoid prosecution from Utah authorities.

**Glendale, UT** Originally called Berryville, this community was abandoned in 1866 because of an Indian uprising. In 1871 the area was reoccupied by displaced people of the Muddy Mission in Nevada and renamed Glendale by their leader, in honor of his birthplace in Scotland.

**Grafton, UT** This community (now a ghost town), settled in 1859, was named in honor of the first settlers' hometown in Massachusetts.

**Harrisburg, UT** Originally called Harrisville, named in honor of Moses Harris, a Mormon pioneer, this community was established in 1859. The name changed to Harrisburg when the township was relocated to better utilize the waters from Quail and Cottonwood creeks.

**Hatch, UT** Named in honor of its original pioneer, Meltair Hatch, in 1872.

*A monument in Kanab*

**Hurricane, UT** Established in 1905, Erastus Snow named this small town as the result of a survey expedition in 1863, when he was attempting to discover a way to irrigate the valley below with the Virgin River located high on the mesa. During their descent from the mesa, a strong whirlwind removed the cover of their buggy, prompting Snow to say, "Well, that was a hurricane! We'll call this the Hurricane Hill."

**Kanarraville, UT** Established in 1861, the community received its name from Ash Creek, which the Paiute Indians called Kanarra Creek.

**La Verkin, UT** Named after the creek that joins the Virgin River west of the area, it is believed that the Paiute Indians corrupted the name given the Virgin River, La Verheen, a Spanish name given to the river by early traders following the Spanish Trail.

**Leeds, UT** A community (now a ghost town) established in the late 1860s, originally called Bennington, in honor of Benjamin Stringham, the local church leader. Stringham later requested the name be changed to Leeds, after Leeds, England, where he had served as a missionary.

**Mount Carmel, UT** Originally called Winsor, in honor of Anson P. Winsor, a Mormon leader living in Grafton, the area was abandoned in 1866 because of the Blackhawk Indian Wars. After residents returned to the area in 1871, the name was changed to Mount Carmel, a town found in Israel.

**New Harmony, UT** Established in 1852, as the first Mormon settlement south of the Great Basin and named in honor of Harmony, Pennsylvania, one of the early centers for the Mormon Church.

**Orderville, UT** Originally referred to as the United Order of Enoch, the area was established in 1874 as part of Brigham Young's experimental socialistic economic system. The residents were to pool their resources for the common good of all. The idea was not widely accepted and in 1875, those who were devoted to the idea formed their own community, Orderville.

**Panguitch, UT** Founded in 1852 by early pioneers who met a band of Paiutes from the paguits or "fisherman" clan of the Panguitch. In the Paiute language Panguitch means "big fish." The area was abandoned due to the Indian wars and resettled in 1871.

**Pintura, UT** Originally called Ashton, then Bellevue, and then changed in 1925 to Pintura, a Spanish word meaning "picture."

**Rockville, UT** Originally called Adventure, located about 1 mile south of its current location, it was established in 1861. Later renamed Rockville, due to the many rocks in the area, when residents were forced to relocate after heavy flooding of the Virgin River.

**St. George, UT** Established in 1861 and named in honor of Mormon apostle George A. Smith, known as the father of the Southern Utah missions.

**Santa Clara, UT** The creek that flows through this area was named by early Spanish explorers, *Santa* meaning "female saint" and *Clara* meaning "short period of good weather." Anglos settled the area in 1854.

**Silver Reef, UT** Established in 1874 when silver was discovered in the sandstone of that area. The mining town boomed for several years until a decline in silver prices forced the abandonment of the area. Today the old ghost town is a popular destination for visitors.

**Springdale, UT** Established in 1862 and located south of its current location, the town was named for the springs that fed a swampy area where residents first settled. Plagued by malaria and the Indian Wars, the township was abandoned and then reoccupied in its current location in 1869 after fears of Indian attacks had subsided and the swamp had been drained.

**Toquerville, UT** Originally occupied by Paiute Indians, led by Chief Toquer (a Paiute word meaning "black," apparently given to the chief because of his dark skin), was occupied by Mormon settlers, with the chief's permission, to share the springs in the 1850s.

**Tropic, UT** Established in 1892 after residents of the Paria Valley had successfully channeled water from the Sevier River atop the Paunsagunt Plateau into the valley. The name of Tropic was chosen because the climate there is in such contrast with that on the Plateau.

**Virgin City, UT** Originally called Pocketville, named from the Paiute Indian word for that area, Pockich, meaning cove. Residents changed the name to Virgin City in honor of the nearby river.

**Washington, UT** Established in 1857 as a Mormon settlement to raise cotton and other crops; named in honor of George Washington.

*Prickly pear cactus*

# 14. Plants and Animals of Zion

A wide range of plants and animals call Zion home. With the diversity in elevation, sunny locations, shaded canyons, waterways, and harsh environments, the plants and animals of Zion have adapted by developing functions, structures, or habits of survival for this region. Zion consists of several different life zones or distinctive biotic communities, which play host to different plant and animal life based on available water, type of soils, temperatures, exposure to sunlight, elevation, and competition. Because of the deep canyons of Zion, we find plant and animal life zones vary, based on exposure. For example, because of cool temperatures created by shade from the tall cliffs we

can have plants and animals typically found 3,000 feet higher in these areas than those found across the canyon in sun-exposed areas. Plants are usually the easiest way to determine a life zone. The following is a basic description of the life zones found within Zion, with a general listing of indicator plants and animals in each.

### Lower Sonoran Zone
Elevation of 4,000 feet and lower—Visitor Center Elevation

Here we find the indicator plants to be the creosote bush, rubber rabbitbrush, common sagebrush, and cactus. This area is sometimes referred to as the Snake/Lizard or Desert Dweller Zone.

### Riparian Zone
Streams or Rivers at any Elevation

Indicator plants in the riparian consist of the Fremont cottonwood, river willow, and the tamarisk. Beaver, muskrats, the dipper, and other bird species are found in this zone.

### Upper Sonoran Zone
Elevation of 6,800 to 4,000 feet—Canyon slopes to canyon rim and the east side of park.

The pinyon pine and juniper trees are found in this zone along with animals such as the ringtail cat, porcupine, jackrabbit, rock squirrel, pinyon jay and juniper titmouse.

### Transition Zone
Elevation of 8,000 to 6,800 feet—Canyon rim to Lava Point area.

The ponderosa pine, Gambel oak, serviceberry, and manzanita are found in this zone, along with animals from both the Upper Sonoran and Canadian zone.

### Canadian Zone
Elevation of 9,500 to 8,000 feet—A few areas found in the very north end of the park.

Quaking aspen, blue spruce, and Douglas fir represent this zone along with animals such as prairie dogs, chipmunks, marmots, bear, and elk.

Animals are adaptable to most environments and so most animals could be found within any of the life zones listed above.

*Mule deer having lunch*

# Zion Plant Life

Many plant species thrive in Zion and the different life zones. The unique geology of massive cliffs has created such diverse environments as deserts, swamps, high plateaus, riparian, and hanging gardens.

Because of this diversity in plant communities, 70 percent of all the plants found within the state of Utah can be found in Zion National Park.

## Common Plant Checklist

| | Location | Blooming Season | Flower Color |
|---|---|---|---|
| **Trees** | | | |
| **Birch Family** | | | |
| ☐ Black/Water birch | CA | E/Sp | G |
| **Elm Family** | | | |
| ☐ Hackberry | CT | E/Sp | G |
| **Juniper Family** | | | |
| ☐ Arizona cypress | C | NF | NF |
| ☐ Utah juniper | DTSL | NF | NF |
| ☐ Rocky Mountain juniper | CSL | NF | NF |
| **Maple Family** | | | |
| ☐ Bigtooth maple | CSL | E/Sp | G |
| ☐ Boxelder | CSA | E/Sp | G |
| **Oak or Beech Family** | | | |
| ☐ Gambel oak | CTSL | E/Sp | G |
| ☐ Shrub live oak | DCTS | E/Sp | G |

| | Location | Blooming Season | Flower Color |
|---|---|---|---|
| ☐ Wavyleaf oak | C | E/Sp | G |
| **Olive Family** | | | |
| ☐ Singleleaf ash | CTS | Sp | G |
| ☐ Desert/velvet ash | CA | Sp | G |
| **Paradise Tree Family** | | | |
| ☐ Tree of heaven | C | L/Sp Su | G |
| **Pea Family** | | | |
| ☐ New Mexico locust | C | L/Sp | P |
| ☐ Black locust | C | L/Sp | W |
| **Pine Family** | | | |
| ☐ White fir | CL | NF | NF |
| ☐ Pinyon | CTSL | NF | NF |
| ☐ Single-leaf pinyon | CTSL | NF | NF |
| ☐ Ponderosa pine | SL | NF | NF |
| ☐ Douglas fir | CSL | NF | NF |
| **Rose Family** | | | |
| ☐ Apple tree | C | E/Sp | P/W |
| ☐ Pear tree | C | E/Sp | W |
| **Tamarix Family** | | | |
| ☐ Tamarisk | CA | E/Sp | P |
| **Willow Family** | | | |
| ☐ Fremont cottonwood | CSA | Sp | G |
| ☐ Quaking aspen | SL | Sp | G |
| ☐ Willow | CA | E/Sp | G |

## PLANT LIFE LEGEND

**Location**
D = Desert, lower washes, sandy areas
C = Canyons (all elevations)
T = Talus slopes and mesas
S = Slickrock, cliffs
H = Hanging gardens
A = Waterways, streams
L = Plateaus, high elevation (6300–8700 ft.)

**Blooming Season**
Sp = Spring
Su = Summer
Fa = Fall
Wi = Winter
E = Early
L = Late
NF = Nonflowering

**Flower Color**
R = Red
O = Orange
Y = Yellow
G = Green
B = Blue
V = Violet/purple
P = Pink
W = White

## Shrubs

| | Location | Blooming Season | Flower Color |
|---|---|---|---|
| **Agave Family** | | | |
| ☐ Datil yucca | DCT | Sp E/Su | W |
| ☐ Utah yucca | DCTS | Sp E/Su | W |
| **Barberry Family** | | | |
| ☐ Creeping mahonia or Oregon grape | CL | Sp | Y |
| **Buckwheat Family** | | | |
| ☐ Golden eriogonum | S | L/Su Fa | Y |
| **Cashew/Sumac Family** | | | |
| ☐ Squawbush | DCT | E/Sp | Y |
| ☐ Poison ivy | CHA | L/Sp Su | G |
| **Composite Family** | | | |
| ☐ Old man sagebrush | DCT | Sp-Fa | W |
| ☐ Big sagebrush | DCL | Fa | W |
| ☐ Waterwillow | CA | Fa | W |
| ☐ Rabbit brush | DC | Fa | Y |
| ☐ Broom/Snakeweed | DCT | Fa | Y |
| ☐ Bush encelia | DT | Su | Y |
| **Dogwood Family** | | | |
| ☐ Red-osier dogwood | L | Sp | W |
| **Goosefoot Family** | | | |
| ☐ Four-wing saltbush | DC | Sp | G |
| **Grape Family** | | | |
| ☐ Canyon grape | CA | Sp | G |
| **Heath Family** | | | |
| ☐ Manzanita | TSL | Wi E/sp | P |
| **Honeysuckle Family** | | | |
| ☐ Elderberry | L | Su | W |
| ☐ Snowberry | CL | Sp E/Su | P/W |
| **Joint-Fir Family** | | | |
| ☐ Mormon tea | DCT | NF | NF |
| **Mint Family** | | | |
| ☐ Desert sage | CDT | Sp | V |

| | Location | Blooming Season | Flower Color |
|---|---|---|---|
| **Mustard Family** | | | |
| ☐ Prince's Plume | DCT | Sp | Y |
| **Oleaster Family** | | | |
| ☐ Russian olive | CA | L/Sp | Y |
| ☐ Roundleaf buffaloberry | DT | L/Wi | Y/G |
| **Pea Family** | | | |
| ☐ Indigobush | D | Sp | V |
| **Potato Family** | | | |
| ☐ Wolfberry, tomatilla | DC | Sp | W |
| **Rose Family** | | | |
| ☐ Saskatoon serviceberry | CL | Sp | W |
| ☐ Utah serviceberry | CTL | Sp | W |
| ☐ Mountain mahogany | S | Sp | Y |
| ☐ Blackbrush | DC | Sp | Y |
| ☐ Western chokecherry | L | L/Sp | W |
| ☐ Cliffrose | DCTS | SP | Y |
| ☐ Bitterbrush | CTL | Sp | Y |
| ☐ Woods wild rose | CAL | Su | P |
| **Silk Tassel Family** | | | |
| ☐ Silk tassel bush | C | L/Wi | G |

*Claret cup cactus*

## Herbs

| | Location | Blooming Season | Flower Color |
|---|---|---|---|
| **Bellflower Family** | | | |
| ☐ Cardinal flower | CHA | L/Su Fa | R |
| **Borage Family** | | | |
| ☐ Yellow forget-me-not | TC | E/Sp | Y |
| ☐ Golden cryptanth | DC | Sp | Y |
| ☐ Puccoon | DCTS | SP | Y |
| **Buckwheat Family** | | | |
| ☐ Slickrock Sulfurflower | S | Su Fa | O/Y |
| ☐ Zion desert trumpet | D | Sp–Fa | P/W |
| ☐ White-flowered Thompson eriogonum | C | Fa | W |
| ☐ Wild rhubarb | CD | Sp | P |
| **Buttercup Family** | | | |
| ☐ Golden columbine | CHA | Sp E/Su | Y |
| ☐ Western columbine | CHA | Sp E/Su | R/Y |
| ☐ Larkspur | DCSL | Sp | B/V |
| ☐ Sand buttercup | S | E/Sp | P/W |
| **Cactus Family** | | | |
| ☐ Purple torch | CD | Sp | V |
| ☐ Claret cup | DTS | Sp | R |
| ☐ Utah beavertail | DTS | Sp | P |
| ☐ Cholla | CD | E/Su | Y/G |
| ☐ Engelmann prickly pear | DCT | L/Sp Su | O/Y |
| ☐ Cliff prickly pear | CD | Sp | P |

*Desert star*

| | Location | Blooming Season | Flower Color |
|---|---|---|---|
| ☐ Prickly pear | DCTL | L/Sp Su | R/O Y/P |
| **Caper Family** | | | |
| ☐ Yellow beeplant | DS | L/Sp–Fa | Y |
| **Cattail Family** | | | |
| ☐ Cattail | HA | Sp | G |
| **Composite Family** | | | |
| ☐ Western yarrow | DT | Su Fa | W |
| ☐ Pussytoes | T | Sp | P/W |
| ☐ Tansy aster | C | Fa | V |
| ☐ Glaucous aster | CHA | Fa | V/W |

---

## PLANT LIFE LEGEND

### Location
**D** = Desert, Lower Washes, Sandy Areas
**C** = Canyons (all elevations)
**T** = Talus Slopes and Mesas
**S** = Slickrock, cliffs
**H** = Hanging Gardens
**A** = Waterways, streams
**L** = Plateaus, high elevation (6300–8700 ft.)

### Blooming Season
**Sp** = Spring
**Su** = Summer
**Fa** = Fall
**Wi** = Winter
**E** = Early
**L** = Late
**NF** = Nonflowering

### Flower Color
**R** = Red
**O** = Orange
**Y** = Yellow
**G** = Green
**B** = Blue
**V** = Violet/purple
**P** = Pink
**W** = White

| | Location | Blooming Season | Flower Color |
|---|---|---|---|
| ☐ Siskiyou aster | C | Fa | V/W |
| ☐ Desert marigold | DT | Sp–Fa | Y |
| ☐ Arrowleaf balsamroot | L | Sp | Y |
| ☐ Arizona thistle | DCT | Sp Su | R/O |
| ☐ New Mexico thistle | D | Sp | W |
| ☐ Utah thistle | CT | Sp | P/W |
| ☐ Utah daisy | DCT | Sp | P |
| ☐ Zion daisy | H | Sp Su | W |
| ☐ Sunflower | DCTL | E/Su | Y |
| ☐ Goldenaster | DCSL | SP–Fa | Y |
| ☐ Broom senecio | DCSL | Fa | Y |
| ☐ Goldenrod | CTSL | Su Fa | Y |
| ☐ Wirelettuce | CS | Sp–Fa | P |
| ☐ Goatsbeard | DCL | E/Su | Y |

## Duckweed Family

| | Location | Blooming Season | Flower Color |
|---|---|---|---|
| ☐ Duckweed | HA | Su–Fa | G |

## Evening Primrose Family

| | Location | Blooming Season | Flower Color |
|---|---|---|---|
| ☐ Yellow day primrose | DCTS | Sp | Y |
| ☐ White tufted evening primrose | TS | Sp E/Su | W |
| ☐ Pale evening primrose | DCSL | Sp E/Su | W |
| ☐ Hummingbird trumpet | CSL | L/Su Fa | R |

## Figwort Family

| | Location | Blooming Season | Flower Color |
|---|---|---|---|
| ☐ Early paintbrush | DC | Sp | R |
| ☐ Giant red paintbrush | DC | L/Sp | R |
| ☐ Wyoming paintbrush | DCT | Sp–Fa | R |
| ☐ Slickrock paintbrush | S | Sp | R |
| ☐ Scarlet monkeyflower | CHA | Sp–Fa | R |
| ☐ Eaton penstemon | DCTL | Sp | R |
| ☐ Low penstemon | CL | Sp | B |
| ☐ Jones penstemon | CS | E/Sp Su | R |
| ☐ Royal penstemon | CS | Sp | B/V |
| ☐ Palmer penstemon | DCTL | E/Sp | P |
| ☐ Utah penstemon | CSTL | E/Sp | R |
| ☐ Flannel mullein | CAL | Su | Y |

## Flax Family

| | Location | Blooming Season | Flower Color |
|---|---|---|---|
| ☐ Lewis/blue flax | DCTL | Su | B |

## Four O'clock Family

| | Location | Blooming Season | Flower Color |
|---|---|---|---|
| ☐ Fragrant sand verbena | DCTS | E/Sp–Fa | W |
| ☐ Colorado four o'clock | DCT | E/Sp Su | V |

## Gentian Family

| | Location | Blooming Season | Flower Color |
|---|---|---|---|
| ☐ Elkweed | L | Sp | G/W |
| ☐ Whitemargin gentian | DC | L/Sp | W |

## Geranium Family

| | Location | Blooming Season | Flower Color |
|---|---|---|---|
| ☐ Filaree | CS | E/Sp–Fa | P |
| ☐ Wild geranium | CL | Su | V/P |

## Goosefoot Family

| | Location | Blooming Season | Flower Color |
|---|---|---|---|
| ☐ Russian thistle | DC | Sp | R/G |

## Gourd Family

| | Location | Blooming Season | Flower Color |
|---|---|---|---|
| ☐ Wild or Coyote gourd | DCT | Sp | Y |

---

## PLANT LIFE LEGEND

**Location**
- **D** = Desert, Lower Washes, Sandy Areas
- **C** = Canyons (all elevations)
- **T** = Talus Slopes and Mesas
- **S** = Slickrock, cliffs
- **H** = Hanging Gardens
- **A** = Waterways, streams
- **L** = Plateaus, high elevation (6300–8700 ft.)

**Blooming Season**
- **Sp** = Spring
- **Su** = Summer
- **Fa** = Fall
- **Wi** = Winter
- **E** = Early
- **L** = Late
- **NF** = Nonflowering

**Flower Color**
- **R** = Red
- **O** = Orange
- **Y** = Yellow
- **G** = Green
- **B** = Blue
- **V** = Violet/purple
- **P** = Pink
- **W** = White

*Desert four o'clock*

| | Location | Blooming Season | Flower Color |
|---|---|---|---|
| **Lily Family** | | | |
| ☐ Tapertip onion | CL | Sp | P |
| ☐ Patis onion | L | Sp | P |
| ☐ Benstem mariposa | DCTL | Sp | V/P |
| ☐ Sego lily | CTL | Sp | W |
| ☐ Bluedicks | CTSL | Sp | V |
| ☐ Death camas | DCTL | Sp | W |
| ☐ False Solomon's seal | CHA | Sp | W |
| **Madder Family** | | | |
| ☐ Bedstraw | C | L/Sp Su | W |
| ☐ Madder | C | L./Sp Su | Y |
| **Mallow Family** | | | |
| ☐ Globemallow | DCTS | Sp | O |

| | Location | Blooming Season | Flower Color |
|---|---|---|---|
| **Milkweed Family** | | | |
| ☐ Butterfly milkweed | DC | Sp E/Su | O |
| **Mistletoe Family** | | | |
| ☐ Juniper mistletoe | DTSL | Su | G |
| **Mustard Family** | | | |
| ☐ Rockcress | CTL | E/Sp | P |
| ☐ Chorispora | C | Sp | V |
| ☐ Zion draba | CSL | Sp | Y |
| ☐ Western wallflower | DCTL | Sp | Y |
| ☐ Watercress | HA | Su | W |
| ☐ Twinpod | TL | Sp | Y |
| **Orchid Family** | | | |
| ☐ Giant helleborine | CSHA | Sp | V |

## PLANT LIFE LEGEND

**Location**
- **D** = Desert, Lower Washes, Sandy Areas
- **C** = Canyons (all elevations)
- **T** = Talus Slopes and Mesas
- **S** = Slickrock, cliffs
- **H** = Hanging Gardens
- **A** = Waterways, streams
- **L** = Plateaus, high elevation (6300–8700 ft.)

**Blooming Season**
- **Sp** = Spring
- **Su** = Summer
- **Fa** = Fall
- **Wi** = Winter
- **E** = Early
- **L** = Late
- **NF** = Nonflowering

**Flower Color**
- **R** = Red
- **O** = Orange
- **Y** = Yellow
- **G** = Green
- **B** = Blue
- **V** = Violet/purple
- **P** = Pink
- **W** = White

| | Location | Blooming Season | Flower Color |
|---|---|---|---|
| **Orpine Family** | | | |
| ☐ Stonecrop | S | L/Sp Su | Y |
| **Pea Family** | | | |
| ☐ Stinking milkvetch | DCT | Sp | W |
| ☐ Zion milkvetch | DCT | Sp | V |
| ☐ Zion sweetpea | DCT | Sp | V |
| ☐ Deerclover | DCS | Sp | O/Y |
| ☐ Lupine | DTL | Sp | V |
| ☐ Thompson peteria | DCL | L/Sp Su | W |
| ☐ Sweet-clover | CS | L/Sp Su | Y/W |
| ☐ Utah clover | C | Sp | V/P |
| ☐ Vetch | CT | L/Sp | B/V |
| **Phlox Family** | | | |
| ☐ Skyrocket or scarlet gilia | TL | Sp | R |
| ☐ Arizona skyrocket | D | Sp Su | R |
| ☐ Nuttall gilia | CS | Sp | W |
| ☐ Desert/mountain phlox | CS | E/Sp | R/P |
| ☐ Zion Canyon phlox | C | E/Sp | P |
| **Pink Family** | | | |
| ☐ Sandwort | DSHL | L/Sp Su | W |
| ☐ Common chickweed | DCTS | Sp | W |
| **Pondweed Family** | | | |
| ☐ Leafy pondweed | HA | Su | G |
| **Potato Family** | | | |
| ☐ Sacred datura | DCT | L/Sp–Fa | W |
| ☐ Groundcherry | C | L/Sp Su | Y |
| ☐ Nightshade | DC | L/Sp Su | V |

| | Location | Blooming Season | Flower Color |
|---|---|---|---|
| **Primrose Family** | | | |
| ☐ Zion shooting star | HA | Sp | P |
| **Purslane Family** | | | |
| ☐ Spring beauty | H | Sp | P |
| ☐ Bitterroot | L | Sp | W |
| ☐ Miners lettuce | HA | Sp | W |
| **Rose Family** | | | |
| ☐ Rockmat/Rockspiraea | S | Fa | W |
| **Saxifrage Family** | | | |
| ☐ Alumroot | CSH | E/Su | P |
| ☐ Woodland star | L | Sp | P/W |
| **Spiderwort Family** | | | |
| ☐ Spiderwort | SC | Sp | P/V |
| **Spurge Family** | | | |
| ☐ Whitemargin spurge | SCT | Sp | R/W |
| **Violet Family** | | | |
| ☐ Wanderer violet | HA | Sp | V |
| **Waterleaf Family** | | | |
| ☐ Phacelia | DCL | E/Su | R/O Y/P |
| ☐ Scorpion weed | C | E/Su | W |

## Grasslike Plants

| | Location | Blooming Season | Flower Color |
|---|---|---|---|
| **Grass Family** | | | |
| ☐ Big bluestem | CT | Su Fa | |
| ☐ Purple/red three-awn | CT | Su Fa | |
| ☐ Side-oats grama | CT | Su Fa | |

|  | Location | Blooming Season | Flower Color |
|---|---|---|---|
| ☐ Cheatgrass | DC | Sp | |
| ☐ Jones reedgrass | H | L/Su Fa | |
| ☐ Fescue | CT | Su Fa | |
| ☐ Needle and thread grass | DC | Sp | |
| ☐ Indian ricegrass | DCTS | Sp | |

**Rush Family**

|  | Location | Blooming Season | Flower Color |
|---|---|---|---|
| ☐ Rush | HA | Sp | |

**Sedge Family**

|  | Location | Blooming Season | Flower Color |
|---|---|---|---|
| ☐ Sedge | HA | E/Sp Su | |
| ☐ Bulrush | HA | E/Sp Su | |

## Ferns and Allies

**Fern Family**

|  | Location | Blooming Season | Flower Color |
|---|---|---|---|
| ☐ Maidenhair fern | HA | NF | NF |

**Scouring Rush Family**

|  | Location | Blooming Season | Flower Color |
|---|---|---|---|
| ☐ Meadow horsetail | HA | NF | NF |
| ☐ Scouring rush | HA | NF | NF |

*Clark's nutcracker*

# Zion Bird Life

With the diversity of environments in Zion National Park, many bird habitats are compressed into a small space. If you enjoy bird-watching you should be able to visit Zion's different habitats in just a few hours. Over 290 bird species have been recorded in Zion and about 60 are permanent residents. Use the following bird list and see how many you can identify.

## Zion and Vicinity Bird Checklist

(Information about how common a bird may be is based on sightings during the best time of year to see that particular species.)

|  | Profile | Time of Year | Habitat |
|---|---|---|---|
| **Loons and Grebes** | | | |
| ☐ Common loon | r | Sp/Fa | W |
| ☐ Pied-billed grebe | u | Yr | W |
| ☐ Horned grebe | x | Fa/Wi | W |

---

**BIRD LIFE LEGEND**

**Profile**
c = Common
u = Uncommon
r = Rare
s = Sporadic
x = Chance
* = Breeds in Zion

**Time of Year**
Sp = Spring
Su = Summer
Fa = Fall
Wi = Winter
Yr = Year Round

**Habitat**
D = Desert environment
R = Riparian environment
P = Pinyon and juniper woodland environment
E = Evergreen tree environment
W = Water—rivers, ponds, lakes, etc.
A = Almost any habitat

| | Profile | Time of Year | Habitat |
|---|---|---|---|
| ☐ Eared grebe | c | Sp/Fa | W |
| ☐ Western grebe | r | Sp/Fa | W |
| ☐ Clark's grebe | x | –––- | W |

## Pelicans and Cormorants

| | Profile | Time of Year | Habitat |
|---|---|---|---|
| ☐ American white pelican | r | Fa | W |
| ☐ Double-crested cormorant | r | Sp | W |

## Herons, Ibises, and Storks

| | Profile | Time of Year | Habitat |
|---|---|---|---|
| ☐ American bittern | x | Sp/Fa | W |
| ☐ Great blue heron | u | Yr | W |
| ☐ Great egret | r | Sp | W |
| ☐ Snowy egret | u | Sp | W |
| ☐ Cattle egret | r | Sp/Fa | W |
| ☐ Green heron | r | Sp/Fa | W |
| ☐ Black-crowned night heron | r | Yr | W |
| ☐ White-faced ibis | u | Sp | W |
| ☐ Wood stork | x | Su | W |

## Vultures

| | Profile | Time of Year | Habitat |
|---|---|---|---|
| ☐ *Turkey vulture | c | Su | A |
| ☐ California condor | x | yr | EP |

## Swans, Geese, and Ducks

| | Profile | Time of Year | Habitat |
|---|---|---|---|
| ☐ Tundra swan | x | Wi | W |

*Bald eagle*

| | Profile | Time of Year | Habitat |
|---|---|---|---|
| ☐ Snow goose | r | Sp/Su | W |
| ☐ Canada goose | u | Wi | W |
| ☐ Wood duck | u | Fa–Sp | W |
| ☐ *Green-winged teal | c | Sp/Fa | W |
| ☐ *Mallard | c | Yr | W |
| ☐ *Northern pintail | u | Fa–Sp | W |
| ☐ Blue-winged teal | u | Sp | W |
| ☐ *Cinnamon teal | c | Sp/Fa | W |
| ☐ Northern shoveler | u | Fa–Sp | W |
| ☐ Gadwall | u | Fa–Sp | W |
| ☐ American wigeon | u | Fa–Sp | W |
| ☐ Canvasback | u | Fa–Sp | W |
| ☐ Redhead | u | Sp/Fa | W |
| ☐ Ring-necked duck | c | Sp/Fa | W |
| ☐ Lesser scaup | u | Fa–Sp | W |
| ☐ Oldsquaw | x | Wi | W |
| ☐ Surf scoter | x | Wi | W |
| ☐ White-winged scoter | x | Fa | W |
| ☐ Common goldeneye | u | Fa–Sp | W |
| ☐ Bufflehead | u | Fa–Sp | W |
| ☐ Hooded merganser | r | Fa–Sp | W |
| ☐ *Common merganser | u | Fa–Sp | W |
| ☐ Red-breasted merganser | u | Sp/Fa | W |
| ☐ Ruddy duck | u | Fa–Sp | W |

## Osprey, Eagles, Hawks & Falcons

| | Profile | Time of Year | Habitat |
|---|---|---|---|
| ☐ Osprey | r | Sp/Fa | W |
| ☐ Bald eagle | u | Wi | W |
| ☐ *Golden eagle | u | Yr | DEP |
| ☐ Northern harrier | u | Yr | D |
| ☐ *Sharp-shinned hawk | u | Yr | EPR |
| ☐ *Cooper's hawk | c | Yr | EPR |
| ☐ *Northern goshawk | r | Yr | E |
| ☐ Common black hawk | r | Sp/Su | R |
| ☐ Red-shouldered hawk | x | Su/Wi | R |
| ☐ Broad-winged hawk | x | Sp | R |
| ☐ Swainson's hawk | r | Sp–Fa | DE |
| ☐ Zone-tailed hawk | x | Su/Fa | EP |
| ☐ *Red-tailed hawk | c | Yr | A |
| ☐ Ferruginous hawk | r | Yr | DP |
| ☐ Rough-legged hawk | u | Fa/Sp | D |

| | Profile | Time of Year | Habitat |
|---|---|---|---|
| ☐ *American kestrel | c | Yr | DER |
| ☐ Merlin | r | Fa/Wi | PR |
| ☐ *Peregrine falcon | u | Yr | A |
| ☐ Prairie falcon | r | Yr | DE |

## Pheasants, Grouse, Turkey, and Quail

| | Profile | Time of Year | Habitat |
|---|---|---|---|
| ☐ *Ring-necked pheasant | r | Yr | D |
| ☐ *Blue grouse | u | Yr | E |
| ☐ *Wild turkey | c | Yr | ER |
| ☐ *Gambel's quail | u | Yr | DR |

## Rails and Cranes

| | Profile | Time of Year | Habitat |
|---|---|---|---|
| ☐ *Virginia rail | r | Yr | W |
| ☐ *Sora | r | Yr | W |
| ☐ *American coot | c | Wi | W |
| ☐ Sandhill crane | x | Wi | W |

## Shorebirds

| | Profile | Time of Year | Habitat |
|---|---|---|---|
| ☐ Black-bellied plover | x | Wi | W |
| ☐ Snowy plover | x | Su/Wi | W |
| ☐ Semipalmated plover | r | Sp/Fa | W |
| ☐ *Killdeer | u | Yr | DW |
| ☐ Mountain plover | x | Sp | D |
| ☐ Black-headed stilt | u | Sp | W |
| ☐ American avocet | u | Sp | W |
| ☐ Greater yellowlegs | u | Sp | W |
| ☐ Lesser yellowlegs | r | Sp | W |
| ☐ Solitary sandpiper | r | Sp/Fa | W |
| ☐ Willet | u | Sp | W |
| ☐ Wandering tattler | x | Fa | W |
| ☐ *Spotted sandpiper | u | Sp-Fa | W |
| ☐ Long-billed curlew | x | Sp | W |

| | Profile | Time of Year | Habitat |
|---|---|---|---|
| ☐ Marbled godwit | r | Sp | W |
| ☐ Sanderling | x | Sp | W |
| ☐ Western sandpiper | u | Sp/Fa | W |
| ☐ Least sandpiper | u | Sp/Fa | W |
| ☐ Baird's sandpiper | x | Sp/Fa | W |
| ☐ Pectoral sandpiper | x | Sp/Fa | W |
| ☐ Long-billed dowitcher | u | Sp | W |
| ☐ Common snipe | u | Fa–Sp | RW |
| ☐ Wilson's phalarope | u | Sp | W |
| ☐ Red-necked phalarope | r | Sp/Fa | W |
| ☐ Red phalarope | x | Sp | W |

## Gulls and Terns

| | Profile | Time of Year | Habitat |
|---|---|---|---|
| ☐ Franklin's gull | r | Sp | W |
| ☐ Bonaparte's gull | x | Sp/Fa | W |
| ☐ Ring-billed gull | u | Sp | W |
| ☐ California gull | u | Sp | W |
| ☐ Herring gull | x | Fa–Sp | W |
| ☐ Caspian tern | x | Sp/Fa | W |
| ☐ Forster's tern | r | Sp | W |
| ☐ Black tern | x | Su | W |

## Pigeons and Doves

| | Profile | Time of Year | Habitat |
|---|---|---|---|
| ☐ Rock pigeon | r | Yr | DR |
| ☐ *Band-tailed pigeon | u | Su | E |
| ☐ White-winged dove | x | Sp | R |
| ☐ *Morning dove | c | Sp/Su | A |
| ☐ Inca dove | x | Yr | R |

## Cuckoos and Roadrunners

| | Profile | Time of Year | Habitat |
|---|---|---|---|
| ☐ Yellow-billed cuckoo | r | Su/Fa | R |
| ☐ Greater roadrunner | u | Yr | D |

---

## BIRD LIFE LEGEND

**Profile**
- c = Common
- u = Uncommon
- r = Rare
- s = Sporadic
- x = Chance
- * = Breeds in Zion

**Time of Year**
- Sp = Spring
- Su = Summer
- Fa = Fall
- Wi = Winter
- Yr = Year Round

**Habitat**
- D = Desert environment
- R = Riparian environment
- P = Pinyon and juniper woodland environment
- E = Evergreen tree environment
- W = Water—rivers, ponds, lakes, etc.
- A = Almost any habitat

| | Profile | Time of Year | Habitat |
|---|---|---|---|
| **Owls** | | | |
| ☐ Barn owl | r | Yr | PR |
| ☐ *Flammulated owl | r | Sp–Fa | EP |
| ☐ *Western screech-owl | u | Yr | ER |
| ☐ *Great horned owl | u | Yr | A |
| ☐ *Northern pygmy-owl | u | Yr | EPR |
| ☐ *Spotted owl | u | Yr | E |
| ☐ Long-eared owl | x | Sp | DP |
| ☐ Short-eared owl | x | Su | P |
| ☐ Northern saw-whet owl | s | Yr | ER |
| **Goatsuckers** | | | |
| ☐ Lesser nighthawk | r | Su | D |
| ☐ Common nighthawk | u | Sp–Fa | A |
| ☐ *Common poorwill | u | Sp–Fa | DEP |
| ☐ Whip-poor-will | r | Sp | R |
| **Swifts** | | | |
| ☐ Black swift | r | Sp/Fa | R |
| ☐ Vaux's swift | x | Sp/Fa | R |
| ☐ *White-throated swift | c | Sp–Fa | A |
| **Hummingbirds** | | | |
| ☐ Broad-billed hummingbird | x | Fa | R |
| ☐ Blue-throated hummingbird | x | Su | R |
| ☐ Magnificent hummingbird | x | Sp/Su | R |
| ☐ *Black-chinned hummingbird | c | Sp–Fa | A |
| ☐ *Costa's hummingbird | u | Sp | D |
| ☐ Anna's hummingbird | x | Sp/Su | DR |
| ☐ Calliope hummingbird | R | Sp/Fa | ER |
| ☐ *Broad-tailed hummingbird | u | Sp–Fa | E |
| ☐ Rufous hummingbird | u | Fa | ER |
| **Kingfishers** | | | |
| ☐ *Belted kingfisher | u | Yr | RW |
| **Woodpeckers** | | | |
| ☐ Lewis' woodpecker | r | Fa/Wi | E |
| ☐ Acorn woodpecker | r | Sp | E |
| ☐ *Red-naped sapsucker | c | Sp/Fa | EPR |
| ☐ Williamson's sapsucker | r | Fa/Wi | EP |

| | Profile | Time of Year | Habitat |
|---|---|---|---|
| ☐ Ladder-backed woodpecker | r | Yr | DR |
| ☐ *Downy woodpecker | u | Yr | EPR |
| ☐ *Hairy woodpecker | c | Yr | EPR |
| ☐ Three-toed woodpecker | x | Yr | P |
| ☐ *Northern flicker | c | Wi | EPR |
| **Flycatchers** | | | |
| ☐ *Olive-sided flycatcher | u | Sp–Fa | E |
| ☐ *Western wood-pewee | c | Su | ER |
| ☐ *Willow flycatcher | r | Sp/Su | R |
| ☐ Hammond's flycatcher | r | Sp/Fa | ER |
| ☐ *Dusky flycatcher | u | Sp–Fa | EPR |
| ☐ *Gray flycatcher | u | Sp/Su | P |
| ☐ *Cordilleran flycatcher | u | Sp/Su | ER |
| ☐ *Black phoebe | u | Yr | R |
| ☐ Eastern phoebe | x | Sp/Fa | R |
| ☐ *Say's phoebe | c | Sp–Fa | DR |
| ☐ Vermilion flycatcher | x | Sp/Su | R |
| ☐ *Ash-throated flycatcher | c | Su | EPR |
| ☐ *Cassin's kingbird | u | Sp/Su | PR |
| ☐ *Western kingbird | c | Sp/Su | DR |
| ☐ Eastern kingbird | x | Sp/Fa | PR |
| **Shrikes** | | | |
| ☐ Northern shrike | r | Wi | D |
| ☐ Loggerhead shrike | r | Fa–Sp | DE |
| **Vireos** | | | |
| ☐ *Bell's vireo | r | Su | R |
| ☐ *Gray vireo | u | Sp/Su | P |
| ☐ *Plumbeous vireo | c | Sp–Fa | ER |
| ☐ * Warbling vireo | c | Sp–Fa | ER |
| **Jays and Crows** | | | |
| ☐ Gray jay | x | Wi | P |
| ☐ *Steller's jay | c | Yr | EPR |
| ☐ * Western scrub-jay | c | Yr | PR |
| ☐ *Pinyon jay | u | Yr | P |
| ☐ Clark's nutcracker | r | Fa-Sp | E |
| ☐ Black-billed magpie | x | Wi/Sp | DP |
| ☐ American crow | r | Yr | PR |
| ☐ *Common raven | c | Yr | A |

| | Profile | Time of Year | Habitat |
|---|---|---|---|
| **Larks** | | | |
| ☐ Horned lark | u | Wi | D |
| **Swallows** | | | |
| ☐ *Tree swallow | c | Sp/Su | EW |
| ☐ *Violet-green swallow | c | Sp-Fa | A |
| ☐ *Northern rough-winged swallow | c | Sp | RW |
| ☐ Bank swallow | r | Sp | RW |
| ☐ *Cliff swallow | u | Sp–Fa | DW |
| ☐ Barn swallow | r | Sp/Fa | DW |
| **Chickadees, Titmice, and Bushtits** | | | |
| ☐ *Black-capped chickadee | c | Yr | EPR |
| ☐ *Mountain chickadee | c | Yr | EPR |
| ☐ *Juniper titmouse | c | Yr | P |
| ☐ Verdin | x | Fa/Wi | D |
| ☐ *Bushtit | c | Yr | DEP |
| **Nuthatches and Creepers** | | | |
| ☐ *Red-breasted nuthatch | u | Su | E |
| ☐ *White-breasted nuthatch | u | Yr | EP |
| ☐ *Pygmy nuthatch | u | Yr | E |
| ☐ *Brown creeper | u | Fa–Sp | EPR |
| **Wrens and Dippers** | | | |
| ☐ *Rock wren | c | Sp–Fa | DP |
| ☐ *Canyon wren | c | Yr | EP |
| ☐ *Bewick's wren | c | Yr | DP |
| ☐ *House wren | c | Sp/Su | R |
| ☐ *Winter wren | u | Wi | R |
| ☐ *Marsh wren | u | Fa–Sp | RW |
| ☐ *American dipper | c | Yr | W |

| | Profile | Time of Year | Habitat |
|---|---|---|---|
| **Kinglets and Gnatcatchers** | | | |
| ☐ Golden-crowned kinglet | u | Wi | EP |
| ☐ Ruby-crowned kinglet | c | Fa–Sp | EP |
| ☐ *Blue-gray gnatcatcher | c | Sp/Su | DP |
| **Thrushes** | | | |
| ☐ *Western bluebird | c | Sp/Fa | DER |
| ☐ *Mountain bluebird | u | Yr | DE |
| ☐ *Townsend's solitaire | c | Sp/Fa | DP |
| ☐ Swainson's thrush | r | Sp | E |
| ☐ *Hermit thrush | c | Su | ER |
| ☐ *American robin | c | Yr | A |
| ☐ Varied thrush | x | Sp | R |
| **Mockingbirds and Thrashers** | | | |
| ☐ Gray catbird | x | Fa/Wi | R |
| ☐ *Northern mockingbird | u | Su | DP |
| ☐ Sage thrasher | r | Sp | D |
| ☐ Brown thrasher | x | Sp/Wi | R |
| ☐ Crissal thrasher | x | Sp/Fa | DR |
| **Starlings** | | | |
| ☐ *European starling | c | Yr | DR |
| **Pipits, Waxwings, and Phainopepla** | | | |
| ☐ American pipit | u | Fa–Sp | D |
| ☐ Bohemian waxwing | s | Wi | R |
| ☐ Cedar waxwing | u | Fa–Sp | R |
| ☐ *Phainopepla | u | Su | DPR |
| **Warblers** | | | |
| ☐ *Orange-crowned warbler | u | Sp-Fa | ER |
| ☐ Nashville warbler | r | Sp/Fa | R |

---

## BIRD LIFE LEGEND

**Profile**
c = Common
u = Uncommon
r = Rare
s = Sporadic
x = Chance
* = Breeds in Zion

**Time of Year**
Sp = Spring
Su = Summer
Fa = Fall
Wi = Winter
Yr = Year Round

**Habitat**
D = Desert environment
R = Riparian environment
P = Pinyon and juniper woodland environment
E = Evergreen tree environment
W = Water—rivers, ponds, lakes, etc.
A = Almost any habitat

| | Profile | Time of Year | Habitat |
|---|---|---|---|
| ☐ *Virginia's warbler | c | Sp/Su | EPR |
| ☐ *Lucy's warbler | c | Sp/Su | R |
| ☐ *Yellow warbler | c | Sp–Fa | R |
| ☐ *Yellow-rumped warbler | c | Sp/Fa | ER |
| ☐ *Black-throated gray warbler | c | Sp/Su | P |
| ☐ *Townsend's warbler | x | Fa | E |
| ☐ Hermit warbler | x | Su | R |
| ☐ *Grace's warbler | c | Sp/Su | E |
| ☐ Black-and-white warbler | x | Sp/Su | R |
| ☐ American redstart | x | Sp–Fa | R |
| ☐ Ovenbird | x | Sp | R |
| ☐ Northern waterthrush | r | Sp | R |
| ☐ MacGillivray's warbler | u | Sp/Su | DRE |
| ☐ *Common yellowthroat | u | Sp | R |
| ☐ Hooded warbler | x | Fa | E |
| ☐ Wilson's warbler | u | Sp | R |
| ☐ Painted redstart | r | Sp | PR |
| ☐ *Yellow-breasted chat | u | Sp | R |

## Tanagers

| | Profile | Time of Year | Habitat |
|---|---|---|---|
| ☐ *Summer tanager | u | Sp/Su | R |
| ☐ *Western tanager | c | Sp–Fa | ER |

## Towhees, Sparrows, and Juncos

| | Profile | Time of Year | Habitat |
|---|---|---|---|
| ☐ *Green-tailed towhee | u | Sp–Fa | DER |
| ☐ *Spotted towhee | c | Yr | EPR |
| ☐ Abert's towhee | r | Fa/Wi | R |
| ☐ *Rufous-crowned sparrow | r | Yr | DP |
| ☐ American tree sparrow | x | Sp/Fa | DP |
| ☐ *Chipping sparrow | c | Sp–Fa | DEP |
| ☐ Brewer's sparrow | c | Sp/Fa | DE |
| ☐ *Black-chinned sparrow | r | Sp–Fa | DP |

| | Profile | Time of Year | Habitat |
|---|---|---|---|
| ☐ *Vesper sparrow | c | Sp/Fa | DE |
| ☐ *Lark sparrow | u | Sp/Fa | DR |
| ☐ *Black-throated sparrow | c | Sp/Su | D |
| ☐ Sage sparrow | r | Fa–Sp | DP |
| ☐ Savannah sparrow | u | Sp | D |
| ☐ Fox sparrow | r | Wi | DR |
| ☐ *Song sparrow | c | Yr | RW |
| ☐ *Lincoln's sparrow | u | Fa–Sp | DER |
| ☐ Swamp sparrow | x | Sp | R |
| ☐ White-throated sparrow | r | Fa–Sp | DR |
| ☐ Harris' sparrow | x | Wi | DR |
| ☐ Golden-crowned sparrow | r | Fa–Sp | DR |
| ☐ White-crowned sparrow | c | Fa–Sp | A |
| ☐ *Dark-eyed junco | c | Yr | A |
| ☐ Chestnut-collared longspur | x | Fa | D |
| ☐ Snow bunting | x | Wi | P |

## Grosbeaks & Buntings

| | Profile | Time of Year | Habitat |
|---|---|---|---|
| ☐ Rose-breasted grosbeak | r | Sp/Su | R |
| ☐ *Black-headed grosbeak | c | Sp/Su | EPR |
| ☐ *Blue grosbeak | u | Sp–Fa | R |
| ☐ *Lazuli bunting | c | Sp–Fa | PR |
| ☐ *Indigo bunting | r | Sp/Su | R |

## Blackbirds, Meadowlarks, and Orioles

| | Profile | Time of Year | Habitat |
|---|---|---|---|
| ☐ *Red-winged blackbird | u | Sp–Fa | RW |
| ☐ *Western meadowlark | u | Sp–Fa | D |
| ☐ Yellow-headed blackbird | r | Sp/Fa | RW |
| ☐ Rusty blackbird | x | Su | W |
| ☐ *Brewer's blackbird | u | Sp–Fa | ER |
| ☐ Great-tailed grackle | r | Sp/Su | DR |
| ☐ *Brown-headed cowbird | c | Sp/Su | A |

## BIRD LIFE LEGEND

**Profile**
- c = Common
- u = Uncommon
- r = Rare
- s = Sporadic
- x = Chance
- * = Breeds in Zion

**Time of Year**
- Sp = Spring
- Su = Summer
- Fa = Fall
- Wi = Winter
- Yr = Year Round

**Habitat**
- D = Desert environment
- R = Riparian environment
- P = Pinyon and juniper woodland environment
- E = Evergreen tree environment
- W = Water—rivers, ponds, lakes, etc.
- A = Almost any habitat

| | Profile | Time of Year | Habitat |
|---|---|---|---|
| ☐ Hooded oriole | r | Sp/Su | R |
| ☐ *Bullock's oriole | c | Sp/Su | R |
| ☐ Scott's oriole | r | Sp/Su | DP |

**Finches**

| | | | |
|---|---|---|---|
| ☐ Gray-crowned rosy-finch | s | Wi | DP |
| ☐ Pine grosbeak | x | Wi/Sp | E |
| ☐ *Cassin's finch | u | Sp–Fa | DE |
| ☐ *House finch | c | Yr | DPR |
| ☐ *Red crossbill | s | Yr | E |
| ☐ *Pine siskin | u | Fa–Sp | EPR |
| ☐ *Lesser goldfinch | c | Sp–Fa | A |
| ☐ American goldfinch | u | Fa–Sp | DR |
| ☐ Evening grosbeak | s | Yr | ER |

**Weaver Finches**

| | | | |
|---|---|---|---|
| ☐ *House sparrow | c | Yr | DR |

*American dipper*

# Zion Mammal Life

Everyone enjoys seeing animals and those who visit Zion are likely to see at least some of the mammals that call Zion home. However, because of the desert (hot) environment, many of the mammals have adapted by becoming nocturnal, and coming out only after dark in order to avoid the heat. Everyone should understand that wild animals can be dangerous and unpredictable and that getting too close or bothering the animals could be hazardous. Feeding animals is strictly forbidden for the safety of the animal and humans alike. Animals bite and can become sick or even die as a result of being fed by humans. Enjoy the animals, but please be careful and mindful of the fact they are indeed wild and need to remain that way.

## Zion Mammal Checklist

| | Profile | Habitat |
|---|---|---|
| **Shrews** | | |
| ☐ Merriam's shrew | r | D |
| ☐ Montane shrew | u | E |
| ☐ Water shrew | u | W |
| ☐ Desert shrew | u | D |
| **Bats** | | |
| ☐ California myotis | c | E |
| ☐ Western small-footed myotis | c | E |
| ☐ Long-eared myotis | u | A |
| ☐ Little brown bat | u | PE |
| ☐ Fringed myotis | u | A |

---

## MAMMAL LIFE LEGEND

**Habitat**

**D** = Desert or lower elevation
**P** = Pinyon & juniper woodland environment
**E** = Evergreen pine or high elevation
**W** = Water—rivers, ponds, lakes, etc.
**A** = Found throughout the park

**Profile**

**c** = Commonly seen
**f** = Fairly common
**u** = Uncommon
**r** = Rarely seen

| | Profile | Habitat |
|---|---|---|
| ☐ Long-legged myotis | c | A |
| ☐ Yuma myotis | c | A |
| ☐ Western red bat | u | PE |
| ☐ Hoary bat | u | PE |
| ☐ Silver-haired bat | c | E |
| ☐ Western pipistrelle | c | D |
| ☐ Big brown bat | c | D |
| ☐ Spotted bat | u | A |
| ☐ Townsend's big-eared bat | u | A |
| ☐ Allen's big-eared bat | u | E |
| ☐ Pallid bat | c | D |
| ☐ Brazilian free-tailed bat | u | A |
| ☐ Big free-tailed bat | u | A |

## Pika, Rabbits, and Hares

| | Profile | Habitat |
|---|---|---|
| ☐ American pika | u | E |
| ☐ Desert cottontail | c | D |

*Coyote*

| | Profile | Habitat |
|---|---|---|
| ☐ Mountain cottontail | u | PE |
| ☐ Black-tailed jackrabbit | f | A |

## Rodents

| | Profile | Habitat |
|---|---|---|
| ☐ Cliff chipmunk | f | P |
| ☐ Least chipmunk | f | E |
| ☐ Uinta chipmunk | f | E |
| ☐ Yellow-bellied marmot | u | PE |
| ☐ White-tailed antelope squirrel | c | D |
| ☐ Golden-mantled ground squirrel | u | E |
| ☐ Rock squirrel | c | A |
| ☐ Red squirrel | c | A |
| ☐ Northern flying squirrel | u | E |
| ☐ Botta's pocket gopher | c | D |
| ☐ Northern pocket gopher | f | E |
| ☐ Great Basin pocket mouse | u | PE |
| ☐ Long-tailed pocket mouse | u | D |
| ☐ Merriam's kangaroo rat | c | D |
| ☐ Chisel-toothed kangaroo rat | u | D |
| ☐ Ord's kangaroo rat | u | P |
| ☐ American beaver | f | W |
| ☐ Western harvest mouse | c | A |
| ☐ Brush mouse | c | DP |
| ☐ Canyon mouse | c | DP |
| ☐ Cactus mouse | c | DP |
| ☐ Deer mouse | c | A |
| ☐ Pinyon mouse | c | P |
| ☐ Northern grasshopper mouse | u | P |
| ☐ Southern grasshopper mouse | u | D |
| ☐ Bushy-tailed woodrat | u | E |
| ☐ Desert woodrat | c | DP |
| ☐ House mouse | u | D |
| ☐ Long-tailed vole | f | E |
| ☐ Montane vole | f | E |
| ☐ Common muskrat | u | W |
| ☐ Common porcupine | f | A |

## Carnivores

| | Profile | Habitat |
|---|---|---|
| ☐ Coyote | f | A |
| ☐ Kit fox | r | D |
| ☐ Red fox | r | E |
| ☐ Common gray fox | f | DP |
| ☐ Black bear | r | E |

*Desert bighorn ram*

|  | Profile | Habitat |
|---|---|---|
| ☐ Ringtail cat | c | A |
| ☐ Ermine | u | E |
| ☐ Raccoon | u | D |
| ☐ Long-tailed weasel | u | A |
| ☐ American badger | u | A |
| ☐ Western spotted skunk | u | D |
| ☐ Striped skunk | c | A |
| ☐ Mountain lion (cougar) | f | A |
| ☐ Bobcat | u | A |

### Even-toed Ungulates

|  | Profile | Habitat |
|---|---|---|
| ☐ Elk | r | E |
| ☐ Mule deer | c | A |
| ☐ Desert bighorn sheep | u | PE |

## MAMMAL LIFE LEGEND

**Habitat**

**D** = Desert or lower elevation

**P** = Pinyon and juniper woodland environment

**E** = Evergreen pine or high elevation

**W** = Water—rivers, ponds, lakes, etc.

**A** = Found throughout the park

**Profile**

**c** = Commonly seen

**f** = Fairly common

**u** = Uncommon

**r** = Rarely seen

# Zion Amphibians and Reptile Life

In Zion you can find a wide variety of amphibians and reptiles with the most visible being the lizards. Use the following checklist to see how many you can find.

## Reptile Checklist

☐ **Utah banded gecko** Medium sized lizard (2–6 inches), light tan with large eyes and dark crossbands, most evident in the young, becoming blotches as they reach adulthood.

☐ **Collared lizard** Olive, brown, or green with two black bands on shoulder and neck (3–5 inches), tail may be twice the length of body.

☐ **Leopard lizard** Large, slender body (3–6 inches), gray or brown with dark spots on body and tail. White crossbars on back and tail. Gravid females have bright red-orange spots.

☐ **Western chuckwalla** Large potbellied (5–8 inches) lizard, loose folds of skin around neck and on the sides. Males have dark heads with red, yellow, or gray toward the tail. Females tend to be gray with cross-banding.

☐ **Yellowback spiny lizard** Stout, rough-scaled lizard (3–6 inches), yellow, brown, or gray with black shoulder markings.

☐ **Eastern fence lizard** Brown, rusty, or gray (1.5–3.5 inches), yellow or green blotches and there may be some blue on the throat.

☐ **Northern sagebrush lizard** A very spiny lizard, gray, green, or brown (1.5–3 inches), some dark spots and possibly some orange on the forelegs.

☐ **Side-blotched lizard** A small lizard (1.5–2.5 inches), gray or brown with a black armpit. Back pattern of blotches, spots, or speckles.

☐ **Northern tree lizard** Brown to gray (1.5–2.5 inches), fold across throat with band of larger scales down middle of the back.

☐ **Short-horned lizard** Broad, flat body, head crowned by spines (1.5–4.5 inches), gray, yellow, or reddish-brown. Dark brown spots down the back.

*Leopard lizard*

☐ **Northern desert horned lizard** Broad, flat body (2.5–4 inches), similar to Short-horned with one distinct difference—long head spines.

☐ **Western whiptail** Slender, and streamlined (2.5–4 inches), gray or brown with stripes, blotches, or spotting. Juveniles have a bright blue tail.

☐ **Plateau striped whiptail** Slender with dark and light stripes down the back (2.5–4 inches). The throat is white or blue-white and the chin is blue-green.

☐ **Great Basin skink** Long, rounded body with four stripes running down the back (2–4 inches). Light brown with broad brown band on back. Juveniles have bright blue tail.

☐ **Wandering garter snake** Usually gray-green with yellow stripes (18–40 inches); can have varied colors. Usually has well-defined back stripe.

☐ **Regal ringneck snake** A small slender snake (8–30 inches); olive with yellow-orange belly; no ring around the neck.

☐ **Red coachwhip snake** Slender, fast moving, and has a long tail (36–72 inches). May be pinkish or light brown with dark banding on the neck.

☐ **Desert striped whipsnake** Long, slender, and fast moving (36–72 inches). Black or brown body with four stripes running down the length of the body.

☐ **Mojave patch-nose snake** Gray or tan body with triangular scale curved over snout. A dark stripe runs the length of its body on each side.

☐ **Great Basin gopher snake** Large and powerful (36–72 inches) with a small head. Yellowish-gray to reddish-brown; dark blotches down the back.

☐ **California kingsnake** Large (30–60 inches), black and white bands down entire length of body.

☐ **Sonoran mountain kingsnake** A tricolored snake (18–41 inches) with red, black, and white bands covering the length of its body. Black bands border red bands.

☐ **Ground snake** A tiny, glossy snake (8–18 inches), red and black bands that fade into the yellow sides.

☐ **Desert night snake** A slender snake (12–26 inches), gray or tan with dark spots and dark splotch on both sides of the neck.

☐ **Sonoran lyre snake** A slim, cat-eyed snake (18–48 inches); gray with brown blotches edged in black. Broad head with lyre-shaped mark.

☐ **Great Basin rattlesnake** A wide flat head (15–65 inches); gray or brown with dark blotches down the back and a rattle on tail.

## Amphibian Checklist

☐ **Arizona tiger salamander** Large, stocky salamander (3–6.5 inches), yellow or dark olive spots with irregular edges.

☐ **Great Basin spadefoot toad** Stout toad (1.5–2 inches) with a wedge-shaped spade on its hind feet. Olive in color with many small reddish warts, white belly.

☐ **Red-spotted toad** Small toad (1.5–3 inches) with flattened head and pointed snout, olive skin with reddish warts.

☐ **Arizona toad** Medium-sized toad with olive, brown, or pink skin. V-shaped stripe across head, the parotoid glands are oval and widely separated; warts are red or brown.

☐ **Canyon tree frog** Plump and warted (1.5–2.5 inches), Olive, brown, or gray with darker blotches on back. Underside of thigh orange or yellow.

☐ **Northern leopard frog** Slender frog (2–4.5 inches), green or brown with large dark spots and white stripe on upper jaw.

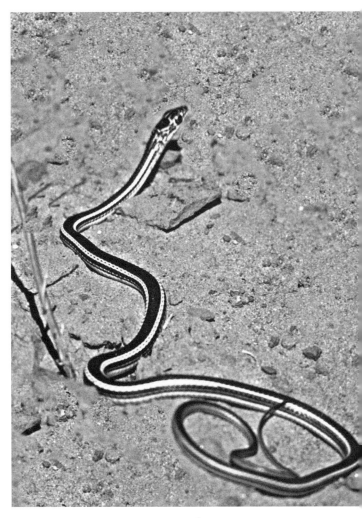

*Common garter snake*

# Index